D0367927

The Baskets
of
Rural America

GLORIA ROTH TELEKI

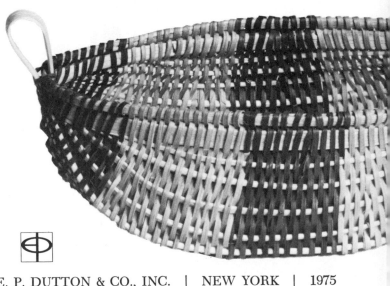

E. P. DUTTON & CO., INC. | NEW YORK | 1975

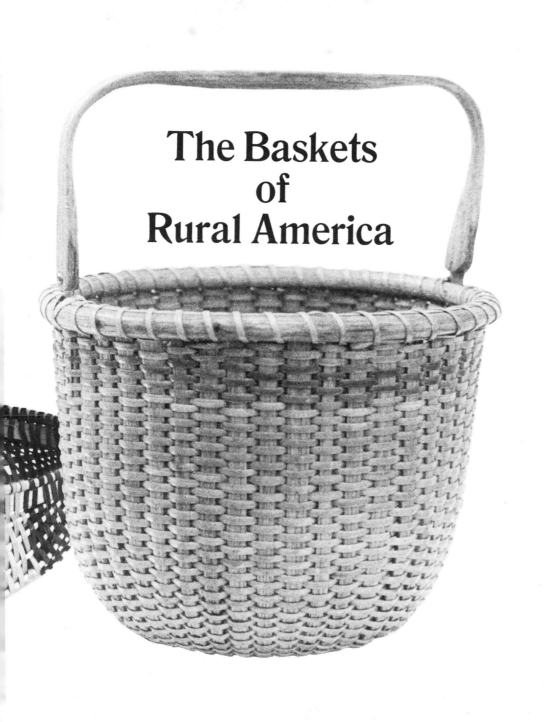

The Baskets
of
Rural America

Excerpt from *Baskets as Textile Art* by Ed Rossbach quoted on page 15 is reprinted by courtesy of Van Nostrand Reinhold Company. © 1973 Studio Vista.

Excerpt from *Two Hundred Years of North American Indian Art* by Norman Feder quoted on page 43 is reprinted by permission of Praeger Publishers. © 1971 by the Whitney Museum of American Art.

Copyright © 1975 by Gloria Roth Teleki
All rights reserved. Printed in the U.S.A.

First Edition

10 9 8 7 6 5 4 3 2 1

No part of this publication may be reproduced or transmitted in any form or by any means, electronic or mechanical, including photocopy, recording, or any information storage and retrieval system now known or to be invented, without permission in writing from the publishers, except by a reviewer who wishes to quote brief passages in connection with a review written for inclusion in a magazine or newspaper or broadcast.

Published simultaneously in Canada by Clarke, Irwin & Company Limited, Toronto and Vancouver.

Library of Congress Catalog Card Number: 75-10075
ISBN 0-525-06140-1 (Cloth)
ISBN 0-525-47409-9 (DP)
Designed by The Etheredges

To Deneb

Contents

List of Figures
and Plates

NOTE: Dimensions given in the plate captions include measurements taken at the widest point, usually at the rim. Height normally includes rigid handles, in which case it is given as O.H. for overall height, and excludes movable handles. D. means height of open basket without a handle. H. includes any cover. Museum-supplied measurements may vary from this pattern.

Plate

Preface

This is a first book on baskets—for the author, who researched and wrote the book she couldn't buy, as well as being the first volume dealing exclusively with the broad range and varied forms of hand-woven American gathering, carrying and storage baskets. Most are from that relatively recent past when America was predominantly rural, but due attention will be paid to the products of today's artisans working within the traditional medium.

The inadequate printed material in the field, mostly a chapter, article, or reference here or there on some particular regional or ethnic area, led to extensive correspondence and footwork to locate and study collections and to speak with knowledgeable informants. It may be a truism that research is never completed, only broken off at some point, as mine has had to be in each of the categories set out here. In some instances I have had to shake out and sift conflicting bits of information as well as I could, and I apologize if my text seems sometimes to be flying in the face of the good advice offered by any of the interested people listed in the Acknowledgments. I must agree with a writer who suggested refraining from overuse of the phrase "in my opinion" or its numerous equivalents, since a work itself entirely represents the substance of its author's opinions.

This volume has been written for both the serious collector and one with some odds and ends of baskets who wants to know more about the things he's been picking up from time to time; the curator awash in unidentified material; the dealer who genuinely likes baskets but is buying to sell ("I can't keep them all!"); the householder furnishing with country things; the interior designer who uses baskets for interest and convenience; and the enthusiast—perhaps a craftworker—for handmade objects. I hope it may prove a source of pleasure, too, for the reader content to house his or her collection within these pages.

Acknowledgments

I should like to recognize the contributions to this book of literally hundreds of interested people: curators, collectors, antiques dealers, basketmakers, librarians, and, chiefly through their publications, earlier researchers in the field. The limitations of space being what they are, and the first draft of this list having proven to be of formidable length, I shall need to single out those participants who are especially to be credited.

Since I cannot include here all the staff members contacted at the Smithsonian Institution, Colonial Williamsburg, The Henry Francis du Pont Winterthur Museum, and numerous others, I shall limit myself to naming only the following curatorial personnel, many of whom personally spent time with me: Dr. John A. Burrison, Director, Museum of Georgia Folk Culture, Georgia State University, Atlanta; Claire Conway, Schwenkfelder Library, Pennsburg, Pennsylvania; Lois R.

Dater, Curator, The Stamford Historical Society, Inc., Stamford, Connecticut; Dr. Frederick J. Dockstader, Director, Museum of the American Indian, Heye Foundation, New York; Henry J. Harlow, Chief Curator, Old Sturbridge Village, Sturbridge, Massachusetts; Carroll J. Hopf, Director, Pennsylvania Farm Museum of Landis Valley, Lancaster, Pennsylvania; Helen Inglis, Curator, Sandwich Historical Society, Center Sandwich, New Hampshire; Dr. Theodore E. Johnson, Director, and David W. Serette, The Shaker Museum, Sabbathday Lake, Maine; C. R. Jones, Associate Curator, New York State Historical Association, Cooperstown, New York; Dr. Rodney L. Leftwich, Department Head, Dept. of Industrial Education and Technology, Western Carolina University, Cullowhee, North Carolina; Betty I. Madden, Curator of Art, Illinois State Museum, Springfield, Illinois; Del McBride, Curator, State Capitol Museum, Olympia, Washington; Robert F. W. Meader, Director, The Shaker Museum, Old Chatham, New York; John Harlow Ott, Director-Curator, Hancock Shaker Village, Pittsfield, Massachusetts; Lester F. Pross, Chairman, Art Department, Berea College, Berea, Kentucky; Lonn Taylor, Director, Winedale Inn, Round Top, Texas; Joseph B. Zywicki, Museum Curator, and Teresa Krutz, Chicago Historical Society, Chicago, Illinois.

I should like to thank the institutions, authors, or publishers, and their photographers and subjects for the figures and plates so identified. William Powers of Twin Lakes, Wisconsin, took the photos of specimens from dealers Lawrence E. King, Monroe Center, Illinois, and Betty Sterling, Brainstorm Farm Antiques, Randolph, Vermont. Plates 27 and 38 are by Helga Photo Studio, New York City. The others, of baskets from several private collections, and the color covers were photographed by Nelson D. (Dave) Rodelius and staff of E.P.S. Studios in Evanston, Illinois, whose competence and perfectionist's eye produced clearly detailed shots of objects that might otherwise have appeared as mere blobs.

I am grateful to my many friends among the antiques dealers who have offered information, baskets, and permission for photography, and to all those collectors who gave encouragement and additional opportunity for study. Here, I shall mention the two with whom I have worked most closely, Mildred Heck of Golf and Patricia Hames of Deerfield, both in Illinois.

Among my valued informants have been the following basketmakers (not all are now active and a few only teach): Clarence Baggett, Grandin, Missouri (through his daughter, Carol Gearhart); Roy Black and Purcell Brown, Colonial Williamsburg, Virginia; Ann Bones, Austin, Texas; Philip Dickel, Middle Amana, Iowa; Carl Ned Foltz, Reinholds, Pennsylvania; Woody Gannaway, Mountain View, Arkansas; Herschal and Margaret Hall, Mountain View, Arkansas; Leslie and Gussie Jones, Branson, Missouri; Wolfram Krank, Albuquerque, New Mexico; Catherine Candace Laird, Beverly, West Virginia; Wayne Rundell, Brooklyn, Connecticut; Faye Stouff, Jeanerette, Louisiana; Floyd E. Umfleet, Maynard, Arkansas; and Paul F. Whitten, Nantucket, Massachusetts. Perhaps most deserving of regard are the weavers of the fine baskets shown in this volume, several of whom appear in the preceding group.

Robert G. Hart, General Manager of the Indian Arts and Crafts Board of the United States Department of the Interior in Washington, D.C., and Stephen M. Richmond of Cherokee, North Carolina, at present the only Field Representative of the Board, have facilitated contacts, as has Leo Rainey, Area Community Resource Development Agent of the Cooperative Extension Service in Batesville, Arkansas.

Department of Tourism employees of a number of states have sent helpful material, but Tyler Hardeman, Travel Editor for the Arkansas Department of Parks & Tourism at Little Rock, has earned special notice for putting together a package that sent me into that state fully prepared for a research trip.

Directors or managers of craft organizations and outlets who have enabled me to procure specimens and who have supplied data include: Betty DuPree of Qualla Arts & Crafts Mutual, Inc., at Cherokee, North Carolina; Irene Donahue of the Ozark Native Crafts Association, Inc., Brentwood, Arkansas; Marie Kopis of Neah Bay, Washington; Leota

Hickey of Ozark Foothills Handicraft Guild, Heber Springs, Arkansas; and Robert W. Gray, Southern Highland Handicraft Guild, Asheville, North Carolina.

Experts and local specialists like C. Gardner Lane, Jr., of Rockland and Peter Paul Terry of Unity, both in Maine; Pierre Bovis of Santa Fe, New Mexico; Lucia H. Jaycocks of Charleston, South Carolina; Joanna and Norman Schanz of West Amana, Iowa; and David H. Wood of Nantucket and Stockbridge, Massachusetts, generously responded to my inquiries.

I have benefited from the counsel and excellent suggestions of my editor, Cyril I. Nelson. The appropriate presentation of this work by my publishers, E. P. Dutton & Co., Inc., has earned my appreciation.

I should like to acknowledge the support and practical aid extended by my relatives, personal friends, and associates. To my husband Deneb and young son David goes my heartfelt gratitude for their unending assistance and good companionship in basketing.

The Baskets
of
Rural America

Introduction

As soon as man took up the habit of gathering and storing extra food and accumulating goods, he needed containers. And, when he looked about him, wherever he lived, he found plants whose fibers could fairly readily be converted into simple receptacles. So was invented what is probably the oldest indigenous craft anywhere—and everywhere—that man turned his questing head, basketry.

Woven plant fibers, affording strength, lightness, and flexibility, proved useful for clothing, shelter, tools, decoration, and even vehicles (fig. 1), in addition to the usual basketry functions of gathering, transporting, and storing food and material possessions. For the purpose of cutting out our field of interest, this volume will confine itself almost exclusively to the study of handwoven or coiled basketry receptacles (vessels, receivers, holders, containers) from our forty-eight contiguous states. It has not been possible to extend firsthand

1

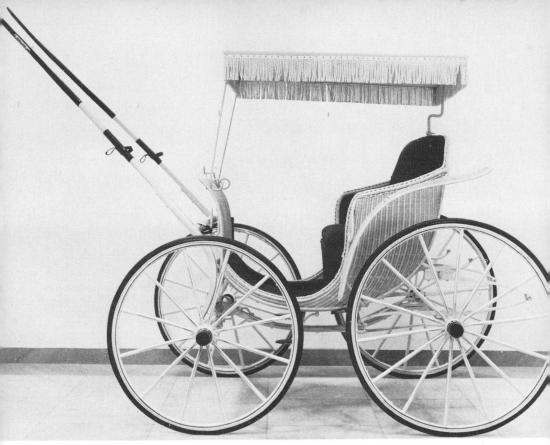

FIGURE 1. Basket Phaeton: c. 1900. The biggest basket of them all! So named for the wicker fenders and riding compartment, its limited maintenance, light weight, and low purchase price made the vehicle very popular. Women proved especially good customers. This beauty has been painted a smashing yellow and is included here strictly for interest. Very early in the nineteenth century, English coachmakers introduced basketry bodies for gigs, considering them the best means to achieve strength without weight. Photograph courtesy the Chicago Historical Society, Chicago, Illinois.

study to Hawaii and Alaska or to the territories of Puerto Rico, the Virgin Islands, and Guam. With the Nantucket Lightship Baskets nearly the only exception, they will be of native materials and made to meet the utilitarian needs of the maker, including that of providing essential or supplemental income from their sale—as opposed to basketry undertaken for its recreational or therapeutic value.

The story of American basketry could not be written without deserved recognition of the outstanding contributions of our native peoples, the original inhabitants of this continent. Not only were they here first, but the American Indian tribes, in their great diversity, made such quantities of baskets, in so many, often complex forms, of an incredible wealth and variety of vegetal materials. Then, too, they were prominent suppliers to the Colonists and pioneers and to the farmers and other rural people who followed them, so that one frequently encounters specimens with construction features intended to satisfy the needs and preferences of non-Indian customers.

Here again, we're obliged to delimit our area for study, so I've opted to include the kinds of traditional baskets Amerinds are still making for their own use today, as well as those originally intended for trade or sale—that is, the kinds of specimens the collector might normally encounter on the market at moderate prices—absolutely leaving the valuable historical, artistic, and ceremonial specimens to earlier researchers. The reader will find some of their most helpful works included in the Selected Bibliography.

One point to be made is that we are concerned throughout with traditional basketmaking. There are artist-craftsmen doing inventive basketwork in the United States today, often with synthetic or at least nontraditional materials. I am thinking of creative people like Wolfram Krank and Ed Rossbach, whose imaginative work is to be found in art museums and private collections. Although their beautiful, original baskets do not fall within the scope of this study and cannot be included, the innovative work, within the traditional medium, of a talented young Ozarker is.

The reader may notice that I do not always name the weavers of new baskets shown, and this has good reasons. One reason is the problem of ferreting out their full names from contacts who are not quite sure or who guard them like state secrets, either out of self-interest or to protect the weavers (many quite elderly) from unwanted pursuit. Another reason involves my own reluctance to start cults of worship of the work of one or another maker.

Sources suggested for older examples and approximations of their dates represent an attempt to be as precise as possible, but the reader will be made aware of the difficulties inherent in or attendant upon attributions.

Our format is to examine origins of the baskets of rural America—ethnic, communal, regional—and to offer identification by tying in the text with a gallery of photographs (the plates at the back of the book) illustrating the range and variations of prevalent forms.

1.

Historical

Before the beginning of the Christian era, there existed in the arid Southwest a people named the Basketmakers by the archaeologists who first uncovered their prehistoric graves. A team had digs in Cliff-Dweller caves in Colorado and Utah in the 1880s and noted that they often encountered deeper burials without pottery but with many baskets, some turned upside down to cover the face. Children were sometimes interred in large baskets.[1] Numerous other sites were excavated, several located in the Four Corners region where Colorado and Utah meet Arizona and New Mexico. They yielded plentiful and highly sophisticated artifacts: coiled baskets, twined bags, human hair cordage, woven sandals, and nets.

The Basketmaker culture has been divided into three periods. What is referred to as the Basketmaker I period, an uncertain number of centuries before the Basketmaker II cave shelters, is assumed, because, although they would have been nomadic hunters and gatherers, the advanced techniques of the artifacts found indicate there had to be earlier development. The Basketmaker II period began with the discovery of corn and the consequent practice of agriculture about the time of Christ's birth. It ended around A.D. 400, when pottery and the circular pit houses representative of the Late Basketmaker, or Basketmaker III, period developed. About A.D. 700 the transition to rectangular stone masonry built above the ground brought the Pueblo period. The combined Basketmaker-Pueblo culture carries the name *Anasazi*.

Actually, radiocarbon-dated artifacts from Danger Cave (named when a rockslide narrowly missed a party of archaeologists), at an elevation of 4,300 feet near Wendover, Utah, prove that North Americans wove baskets at least nine thousand years ago, the earliest known baskets in the world. The Danger Cave basketry consisted of more than a hundred fragments, none larger than a palm, which were found in beds of loess (a wind-formed dust, mostly fine sand and silt) and vegetable matter. These were not burial baskets but were presumed to be the discarded remains of baskets that had been worn to a frazzle. The oldest examples were twined; coiling appeared at the archaeological level above. The techniques could not be identified with specific tribal groups of the region but were at least partly shared by most. Also found at the upper level was an intact net bag of hemp cordage with the fibers still elastic and strong.[2] Such perishable objects cannot survive in open sites, a fact that has obscured basketry's dim beginnings other than under those conditions uniquely favorable to preservation.

However, pottery, once fired, is virtually indestructible. George Wharton James, in the classic *Indian Basketry* (1909, 1972), attests to the antiquity of the craft:

> In the Mississippi Valley, in Arizona, New Mexico and elsewhere in the United States thousands of pieces of pottery have been found which unmistakably show that the soft clay was modelled around the outside or within some basket form which gave the shape of the

vessel . . . It will be observed in studying them that they bear far more impressions of basketry and other textile arts than of natural objects, such as gourds, shells, etc. It is also observable that every basketry stitch or pattern known to the aborigines is found in these pottery impressions. Hence, the natural inferences that basketry antedates pottery, and that the art of basket-making was in an advanced stage whilst pottery was still in its infancy.[3]

Pottery may have been discovered accidentally when clay, used to line baskets so they'd hold water, survived after the basket burned away. Then again, the imprints may have been acquired when the earliest pots were shaped while resting inside a shallow basket base.

There has recently been heightened interest in what are called "temporary" baskets,[4] and the very first baskets must have been such —that is, hastily, or at least casually, contrived on the spot, from whatever vines or other plant materials were at hand, by gatherers or hunters who were lucky enough to make a find and needed an expedient way to transport it. Such containers would most likely have been discarded afterward, a kind of prehistoric equivalent of the throwaway chip or plastic berry boxes we use today.

Among the Native Americans, the need for many containers for various purposes was ongoing: baskets were the cooking "pots and pans" of the Basketmaker II people and the main implements of some historic tribes. Baskets were made at home because everything else was in the self-sufficient Indian family. Elaborate baskets that were honored by being thrown into the fire at the conclusion of funeral or other ceremonies or that were intended as gifts may have been sometime exceptions to the general nonspecialization.

A widespread tradition decreed that the users of implements should be the makers. Since women were assigned the food-preparation and housekeeping chores, they made the baskets and other domestic goods, whereas men made the equipment for hunting and warfare. Tradition dictated exceptions. Among the Pimas, where once an estimated sixty percent of the women could make baskets, men made the burden baskets with saguaro-rib framework and flexible, netlike body of yucca fiber. In general, where both men and women wove, the coarser objects or cruder, heavier baskets would be produced by men. But in the Rio Grande Pueblos, basketry was considered a man's job, other than for certain yucca baskets that were made by women. Iroquois men felled the trees, prepared splint, and carved the handles.

The early immigrants from Europe also found themselves with precious little money for outside purchases. Colonial and pioneer life demanded self-reliance and frugality, and most settlers had to practice many skills well enough to supply almost everything that came to the table, was worn, or was otherwise needed. Frequently, Indians marrying into white families brought basketry skills with them and began a tradition. The exchanges of techniques and designs among natives and newcomers resulted in forms so commingled that, for example, it is impossible to assign either source to a great deal of the utility splintwork from the Northeast.

Basketry lends itself to being a "pickup" or part-time activity. Semiprofessional basketmakers provided supplementary income for the family unit and, of course, professionals came to be established but generally known only in their immediate localities. Basket Street, in the Mount Israel–Guinea Hill section of Sandwich, New Hampshire, is a reminder of a long-ago concentration of weavers there. It had pleasant houses, orchards, and fine hayfields. The basketweavers were good farmers as well; it was usual for artisans to farm, too.

We can trace the prosperity and decline of Dantown, a typical rural community in southwestern Connecticut until it became a bustling basketweaving center in the mid-nineteenth century:

> Gradually its inhabitants began the making of baskets for sale in surrounding townships. By 1860 approximately forty families were engaged in the business. By 1880 the number had doubled, and the trade had become so important that in an area of fifty square miles baskets were used as legal tender. The panic of 1893 marked the beginning of the industry's decline. The next blow came with machine-made baskets, which so decreased business that the younger men, seeing no future in the old craft, sought other work in other localities.[5]

Dantown is now in the north section of Stamford. The Stamford Historical Society has artifacts of Dantown ash-splint basketmaking, including a basket shop's *Day Book of Dann & Curtis* for the years 1851 to 1865. Some 1864 entries follow:

100 bushel baskets	$40.00
105 comen [common] baskets @ $.32	$33.60
100 oyster baskets	$50.00
5 doz. clam baskets	$18.75
12 set[s] large baskets @ $2.50	$30.00
5 doz. peck baskets @ $.20	$12.00
2 doz. fine measuring baskets	$20.00

The firm also made market baskets, cherry baskets, and strappe (strap) baskets, whatever those were. Perhaps the reference was to baskets reinforced with additional splint (or, infrequently, metal) "runners" on the outside to save wear on the bottom; those of splint could be readily replaced when broken. Such a basket is in the society's collection. Or they may have been sowing baskets, some of which were suspended from a strap slipped around the neck, leaving one hand free to steady the basket and the other to broadcast the grain or other seed.

There is a note in the *Day Book* that: "David Deforest commence[d] work July 12th, 1851, @ $25.00 a month." A Stamford photograph (fig. 2) shows a bearded basketmaker, Rezo Waters, seated at work in his shop. His son Ernest stands soaking splints, and several square-bottom-to-round-mouthed baskets and a child are scattered in the foreground.

Since the gathering and preparation of materials is normally more burdensome and time-consuming than the actual weaving, and much of that work can be done by children and shared in by old people, entire families of professionals became common. An interview (through interpreter Alice Bell) with Lela Solomon, a member of the Eastern Band of Choctaws who was born in 1921, appeared in a folder prepared in connection with an exhibition of her work at The State Historical Museum at Jackson, Mississippi, February 27–

March 28, 1971, organized by the Indian Arts and Crafts Board of the United States Department of the Interior in cooperation with the Choctaw Craft Association and the Choctaw Indian Agency. She said:

> When I was growing up, basketmaking was a real family affair among the Choctaws. During the winter months, Mother and Dad, with the

FIGURE 2. Rezo Waters' Basket Shop in Dantown (now north section of Stamford), Connecticut: probably photographed toward the end of the nineteenth century. His son, Ernest, soaks ash splints in what seems to be an inefficiently small tub, but the aim may be to soften just the ends to facilitate insertion. Another son, Rollo (1882–1965), primarily made clam baskets, which were taken by horse and wagon to the Fulton Market in New York City, but also produced handled baskets for flowers, general utility, pack baskets, and others for special orders, all of ash with white-oak frames. The child's identity is uncertain, but he could be a grandson beginning early in the family business. Dantown was a bustling basketmaking center in the mid-nineteenth century, with baskets being used as legal tender within a fifty-square-mile area. Photograph courtesy The Stamford Historical Society, Inc., Stamford, Connecticut.

children helping, would make all kinds of baskets, enough to fill a wagon. When summer came, the family would load up in a wagon, pulled by a team of mules or steers, and travel around the country, for as long as a month at a time, trading baskets for most anything we could get: food, clothing, quilts, and sometimes we could sell a basket for twenty-five cents. This was the family's spending money. After I was married and had my own family to care for, making baskets was the only way I knew to help with the family income to provide some of our needs. There are not many young Choctaw girls who know how to make baskets now, just the older women. I want to see that my people do continue. When the older women are gone, I do not know if it will.

In *Handicrafts of the Southern Highlands* (1937, 1973), Allen H. Eaton tells of Levi Eye, a cheery-looking black weaver from Pendleton County, West Virginia, who supported an extended family of sixteen peddling his split-oak rib-baskets; obviously, Mr. Eye wasn't the only family member working at the craft. Cornelius Weygandt, in *The Dutch Country* (1939), regrets the passing of itinerant basket-making families who could be expected each spring. A Pennsylvania woman told him of such a group, who "camped each year at a good distance from the house and by the stream's side." They had permission to cut their white oak from a stand of trees there, in return for charging half price for the owner's basket purchases.

The author knows of two families weaving baskets today, one doing willow rib-baskets near Pine Mountain, Kentucky, and the other weaving quantities of white oak-splint baskets in northwestern Arkansas. Another Ozarks weaver learned the craft as a young man, when he made his home for several years with a family of basket-makers in Bridgeport, Illinois. His personal files contain clippings and photographs of classes he has taught, a newspaper story telling how he had woven baskets to barter for food after being shot down over Yugoslavia in World War II, and a print showing the weaver with a pickup truckload of a week's work of split-oak baskets that he sold in Fulton, Kentucky, in 1960 at one-fifth of today's prices.

We need to back up a bit now to discuss the rural handicrafts movement, which began toward the end of the nineteenth century and spread to reach its most active growth period during the decade from 1900 to 1910. It was influenced and lent impetus by what has been called the Arts and Crafts Movement in America (1876–1916), which paralleled an English movement and was a kind of reaction against both the less desirable aspects of Victorian taste and the decline of craftsmanship brought about by the introduction of mechanized factory-production methods.

Crafts as recreation came into their own when the country experienced the revival. Some enthusiasts preferred the view of baskets as an art form, as did the Ashley sisters of Deerfield, Massachusetts, who produced a book of instruction [6] containing romantic passages brimming with the joys of working in their "cubby." The most interesting Deerfield baskets were coiled of imported raffia and reed and bore realistic landscape designs, bound in many-colored raffia, around their sides.

The rural handicrafts movement, aided and supported by federal, state, and local agencies, achieved importance in the Southern Appalachian Highlands and was making good progress in New England before being interrupted by World War II. A first National Rural Arts Exhibition, held in the Administration Building of the United States Department of Agriculture in Washington in the winter of 1937, included baskets of local plant fibers from twenty states. Statistics gathered for a study of rural arts and handicrafts in 2,969 counties served by county extension agents in 47 states, Hawaii, and Puerto Rico (California and Alaska didn't participate) for the year 1938 showed 34.7 percent reporting basketwork production of 656,334 units. Basketry followed only needlework and furniture making as an income producer.[7] At the conclusion of World War II, there was renewed activity and interest in encouraging home industries in economically depressed areas and in providing therapy and income for handicapped veterans.

Various guilds and other organizations promoting and selling handworkers' products are active today, but there is little emphasis on basketry. This is simply because the available craftsmen cannot weave as many baskets as could be sold, so the supply continues to fall short of the demand.

NOTES

1. Charles Amsden, *The Ancient Basketmakers*, Southwest Museum Leaflet No. 11 (Los Angeles: Southwest Museum, 1939).
2. Jesse D. Jennings, *Danger Cave*, Anthropological Papers, No. 27 (Salt Lake City: University of Utah Press, October 1957). Also released as Memoir 14, Society for American Archaeology, *American Antiquity*, Vol. XXIII, No. 2, Pt. 2(1957).
3. George Wharton James, *Indian Basketry* (New York: Dover, 1972). An unabridged and unaltered republication of the fourth edition of *Indian Basketry* published in 1909 by Henry Malkan.
4. Ed Rossbach, *Baskets as Textile Art* (New York: Van Nostrand Reinhold, 1973).
5. John V. McClees, "Baskets and Their Making: A Pictorial Demonstration," *Antiques* (May 1931). Reprinted by permission of The Magazine *Antiques*.
6. Gertrude Ashley and Mildred Ashley, *Raffia Basketry as a Fine Art* (Deerfield, Mass.: Published by authors, 1915).
7. Allen Eaton and Lucinda Crile, *Rural Handicrafts in the United States*, Miscellaneous Publication No. 610 (Washington, D.C.: U.S. Department of Agriculture in Cooperation with Russell Sage Foundation, 1946).

2.

Technical

METHODS

The reader may find a bit more in the technical matter here than he or she cares to know, but studying this section will develop the eye for detail, as well as an appreciation of the weaver's problems and skills. Figure 3 illustrates techniques and offers visual exposition for the text.

In *plaiting*, flexible, flat elements—usually of the same size—are interwoven at right angles. *Simple* or *plain plaiting* is also called *checkerwork* or *checker*. Pattern is achieved with *under-and-over* (or *in-and-out*) variations called *twill:* a diagonal pattern, by starting each new row one warp (vertical element) to the right or left, and a zigzag or herringbone pattern by alternating the diagonal movement from one side to the other.

In *wickerwork* (*wicker* or *wicker weave*) the warp or vertical elements are more rigid than the weft or horizontal elements. Commonly, round rods are used, resulting in a considerably stiffer basket. Note that a basket woven of flat strips is considered wickerwork if the warp elements are more rigid.

In *twining* (shown as a form of wicker in fig. 3) two or more flexible elements are interwoven and twisted (that is, turn around each other) between the warps. Twining with the usual two weavers (three or occasionally more may be used) is called *pairing*. The oldest known basketry fragments, those from the Danger Cave site in Utah, were twined at least nine thousand years ago. An excellent discussion of various twining weaves is to be found in *Indian Basket Weaving* (1903, 1971) by The Navajo School of Indian Basketry.

Coiling is correctly referred to as a method or technique, rather than a weave. A foundation that is more or less rigid—a group of rods, a bundle of strands, or a combination of the two—and corresponds to the warp is stitched in a spiraling form. The name *lip-work*, sometimes encountered, derives from the Scandinavian *lob*, meaning coiled basketry.

MATERIALS AND TOOLS

Basketry is a form of textile art that is unlike textile—that is, cloth—weaving in the materials used. Basketry and textile weaving employ the same constructions but differ in that:

> . . . basketry has remained a hand process requiring only the simplest tools, while weaving has been mechanized . . . The fine, pliable, continuous materials of weaving—as opposed to the short, coarser materials of basketry—required the early development of ways to hold them in order without tangling, and ways to facilitate and speed the interlacing . . . The basket is a separate unit, while the piece of weaving can be continuous. The softness of the woven cloth contrasts with the assumed hardness of baskets. Thus baskets, often of so-called hard fibers, are known as hard textiles, although many baskets are soft and pliable . . .

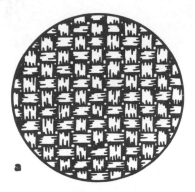

PLAIN PLAITING

TWILL
OVER-TWO-UNDER-TWO

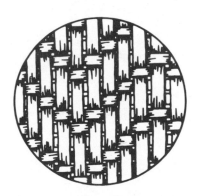

TWILL, VARIED
OVER-THREE-UNDER-ONE

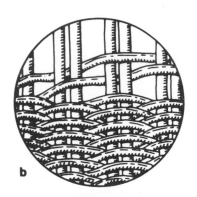

WICKER, PLAIN

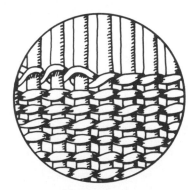

WICKER, TWINED

WICKER, WRAPPED

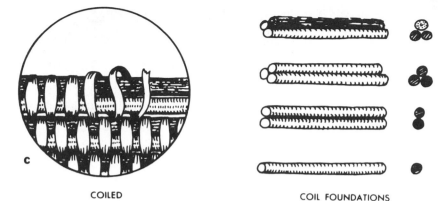

COILED   COIL FOUNDATIONS

Wrapped   Regular Coil Stitch

Herringbone

RIM FINISHES

Techniques for making baskets. (a). Plaiting. Plain plaiting is a simple alternation of elements over and under each other in a simple one-one-one-one rhythm. When the rhythm changes to over-two-under-two or over-three-under-one or some other variation, it is called twilled. It is in twill plaiting that all designing is done in this weave. (b). Wicker weave may be plain: a single element (the weft) woven over and under the stationary "spokes" (warps). Designing is possible when wefts are dyed. The weft can be wrapped around the warp, or double wefts can be alternated in passing over and under the warps entwined about each other. (c). Coiled weave is the most productive of design; it is simply sewing wefts about the warps. The foundation in this weave can be varied: a bundle, two rods and a bundle, or one, two, or three rods. Over the bundle is sewed the weft which may be wider or narrower and the color of which can be changed at any point. *Rims* vary in basketry: they may be simply wrapped, or sewed in the regular coiled stitch, or finished off in a more elaborate herringbone stitch.

FIGURE 3. Techniques for making baskets. Reprinted by permission from *Southwest Indian Craft Arts* by Clara Lee Tanner. Copyright © 1968 by University of Arizona Press, Tucson, Arizona.

These passages, from Ed Rossbach's *Baskets as Textile Art* (1973), do a good job of presenting the distinctions in the close relationship between the two. Another point is the fact that baskets have a "spatial volume."

It will be found that a particular material best lends itself to a certain weave or form. Grasses have been bundled, and coiled baskets have been made throughout the world. But the emergence of the technique in far-flung areas could hardly be considered the result of cultural exchange; rather, it developed separately, as the need to meet the exigencies of handling similar fibers resulted in similar solutions.

American Indians have exploited our native flora to use over one hundred different wild and cultivated fibers for basketry: wood splints, stems and twigs, roots and runners, tree barks, vines, leaves, and grasses. Since twining, a technique heavily used by our first people, involves twisting the elements around each other as they weave under and over the warps, the latter are held firmly in place. It can produce strong, openwork utility baskets of rough fibers or fine, flexible, soft basketry items. Examples of soft materials used in twining are grasses and strands of bark, fern stems, or roots.

Basketry was suited to the nomadic life because it used the passing supply of plants and because a sharp object for cutting them was often the only tool needed. Baskets were light in weight, so they did not add to the wanderer's burden, and they could easily be carried along and finished en route. There was a certain amount of trading for plant fibers not locally available, but basketry generally reflected the plant life of the area, and identification of the fibers in an Indian basket aids in determination of tribal origin.

For the tribes of the harsh Great Basin region (Arizona to Oregon and all of Utah and Nevada) the primary material objects and most important implements were skillfully made baskets. The seminomadic fishing and hunting Plateau tribes (upland Idaho, and Oregon and Washington east of the Cascade Mountains) wove scrub brush and grasses into practically everything they needed. Many coastal tribes, both in the Pacific Northwest and in California, made fine basketry. But it just wasn't needed and didn't develop to any significant extent among the Plains Indians, who found the great buffalo herds a ready source of hides as well as meat. They became adept at tanning and stitched together and decorated remarkable leather storage containers and other necessaries.

There has been much speculation about the origin of North American Indian splintwork, weaving with narrow, flat strips of plant fibers. On the basis of comparisons of cane and wood-splint techniques and examples, many scholars believe that weaving with splints came to the Northern Hemisphere from South America, reaching the Mississippi region, spreading into the Southeast, and reaching the Northeast last. Cane is simple to weave, easily prepared, and sturdy. But it doesn't grow in the Northeast, so wood strips would have been substituted, and the superior splintwork replaced the older birchbark work.[1] We do know, however, that, among the artifacts of the Basketmakers—previous to A.D. 700—of the Southwest, sandals woven of coarse splints of yucca leaves are common. Nine-hundred-year-old ring baskets of plaited yucca-leaf splint are identical to those made today in the Rio Grande Pueblo of Jémez and to the shallower Hopi sifter of plate 22.

In fact, John M. Goggin, writing in an anthropological journal,[2] contends that "plaited twilled basketry was probably widespread over eastern and southwestern United States, much of Mexico, and undoubtedly most of Central America as well," and he points out the necessity for caution "in postulating any historic relationships between South American and southeastern United States basketry other than that both are developments of a basic basketry technique found over much of the New World."

Yet another theory has it that the earliest Indian splint-wood baskets were made in the lower Delaware Valley between 1680 and 1710, where the technique was acquired from Swedish settlers, and that it then spread through New England and Canada around 1750.[3]

Baskets of wood splint are usually of white oak in the Southern

Appalachians and Ozarks and of ash in New England. Older baskets are often of hickory; maple, willow, and other woods have been used but are less satisfactory in handling and durability.

The preparation of splint must be the hardest job in basketmaking. A healthy young tree is carefully selected for size and straightness of trunk and grain. The wood near the ground cannot be used, and the tree should yield a five-to-six-foot log that is relatively free of knots. The log is split into quarters or eighths with a maul and wedges; the outer bark may be removed at this point. A froe (cleaving tool) and mallet are used to divide away the heartwood (sometimes used for splint and often used for ribs and handles) and to split, at right angles to the growth rings, each piece into four. A shaving horse (drawing horse or jack) holds the piece as a drawknife is used to dress (trim) it down to a smooth board as thick as the splints are to be wide.

Splints are then separated by starting them with a knife, following the growth rings and tearing or pulling them apart with the hands; the procedure is repeated until the required thinness is achieved. Torn (rived) splints are stronger and more flexible than those sliced off with some tool because they're made up of long, continuous fibers, that is, the grain has not been crossed. Next, a heavy cloth or piece of leather protects the basketmaker's clothes when scraping and smoothing the splints against the thigh with a knife or shave. Extra smoothness may be had by sanding the finished basket on the outside.

In essence, all that is needed to make a basket are the materials, a cutting tool, and one's hands—the basketmaker's most valuable tools. Many find the work hard on their hands; others do not seem to have as much trouble. They all agree that one needs strong hands to tear splint. The wood must be pliable, so it is woven "green." Old-time basketweavers lived by a stream so that they could throw in the logs to stay fresh and safe from termites and wood beetles. Modern-day weavers are likely to use the logs immediately or to paint the ends so they'll stay fresh in the shade for a month. A pan of water is kept at hand to moisten splint that has dried out, but black ash can be woven dry because it retains its flexibility.

FIGURE 4. "Tools of the Basketmaker," permanent exhibit at the Farmers' Museum, Cooperstown, New York, showing workbench, wooden mold, and a representative set of hand tools. Of course, each craftsman has personal preferences in tools, many of them homemade and traditional in a particular background, so the possible inclusions in a full-range display are legion. At its simplest, basketry requires only suitable fibers, a sharp cutting device, and the hands—the artisan's essential tools. Photograph courtesy the New York State Historical Association, Cooperstown, New York.

Indians of the Northeast pound black ash (called brown ash in some localities) logs all along their length and around their circumference until the growth rings or layers (grains) loosen from each other and separate, an ability characteristic of, and pronounced in, this wood. The wood doesn't come off in sheets, but separates from the log in lengthwise strips, which are then trimmed and split. (White New Englanders also prized black ash, which grew most commonly in the northern half of New England but could be found as far south as Virginia until the supply gave out in many areas.) By 1970 an ash-pounding machine, developed by the University of Maine and a Vista worker, was put into operation among Maine Indian basketmaking groups.

As with any craft, each artisan has his favorite, sometimes home-made, tools. Maine Indians used a "crooked knife" to start splints. Many Ozarks weavers use a homemade two-handled split-cutting knife that is pulled along the edge of a board. Pennsylvania Germans had the *schnitzelbank* or cutting bench to hold the wood in squaring and trimming it with the drawknife. It is possible to saw out basket boards on an industrial band saw if the grain in the tree is quite straight, but sawing actual splints has so far proved unsatisfactory.

Some basketmakers had benches that they straddled, and these might have a spike upon which to impale the bottom of a basket to hold it steady. Figure 4 shows a bench, common hand tools of the basketmaker's trade, and a wooden mold. The Cherokee use crossed sticks to firm the bottom when starting splint baskets, but Amerinds do not seem originally to have woven over molds or forms of any kind. Some non-Indian weavers used pails or wooden forms to enable them to produce splint baskets in exact sizes to use as measures and to obtain symmetrical shapes, and Northeastern Indians took to the use of molds to meet those demands of white customers. Later, neighboring Indians may have brought molds to the Shakers.

An enlightening passage on the coming of technology to the basketmaking Indians of the Eastern Seaboard is contained in Frank G. Speck's *Eastern Algonkian Block-Stamp Decoration:*

. . . newly invented basketmaking tools began to take effect in changing the forms and texture of splint materials in the craft. Ranging between 1850 and 1870, from southern New England to New York State and in Canada, the Algonkian and Iroquois basket-making industry grew sufficiently in importance to stimulate craftsmen of the industrialized groups to produce labor-saving utensils which would enable them to increase the quantity and quality of baskets. The men of all the eastern basket-making tribes were the producers of the total raw materials and builders of coarse baskets; the women were the weavers, designers and finishers of the finer basket creations. Putting thought upon what, by then, had become a profitable home industry to supplant the loss of occupations resulting from the falling-off of the timber industry, hunting, trapping and the older pursuits in general, they devised a series of mechanical inventions. One was a machine to facilitate the riving of ash splints by separating the coarse splints between two boards held between the knees acting like a clamp, and known as a "splitter." Another was the "basket gauge," a hand tool of wood, with a series of sharp teeth usually made of watch springs, across which the broad ribbon-like splint could be drawn, cutting it into finer splints of varying width. The gauge enabled the broad splint of prior use to be reduced to from four to ten strands by one simple motion. Still another innovation in the industry was the solid wooden models or "forms" over which baskets could be shaped as they were built up, to produce uniformity in size and shape in quantity production.[4]

The very names of the inventors had entered into tribal lore.

Indians of the Northeast and Great Lakes region have long woven sweet grass (*Hierochloe odorata,* known by numerous other scientific and common names), a semierect perennial that usually grows in moist places mixed with other grasses and shrubs for shade. It can be propagated from transplants of the creeping rootstocks, but is usually taken from the wild. Before it can ripen, leaves about two-and-a-half feet long are broken off in the ground, then dried slowly in shade or through a speeded-up process using the top of a hot stove. The wonderful scent is due to the presence of coumarin, classed as an essential oil, and it becomes noticeable only upon curing.[5]

Honeysuckle vine, which will grow straight along the ground to great length, was introduced into this country from Japan in the late nineteenth century and spread so amazingly that it is now dispersed throughout the southeastern United States and has reached New England. The Cherokee of North Carolina break off healthy one- or two-year-old stems near the roots, boil them until the bark strips off easily, then smooth them. The Cherokee of Oklahoma substitute buckbrush runners. *Arts and Crafts of the Cherokee* (1970) by Rodney L. Leftwich contains excellent photographs and text covering the preparation of splint and other materials and the construction techniques practiced by the Eastern Band.

Some of the Pennsylvania Germans specialized in wickerwork baskets of willow, frequently growing their own basket willows, of which there are several varieties. A suitably moist patch of ground had to be cleaned and prepared, cuttings planted and pruned back each spring to a foot above the ground, and a mature, five-year-old stump yielded annually up to twenty osiers, each two-and-a-half to twelve feet in length. If allowed to dry, they had to be soaked in warm water to regain pliability. The varying thicknesses sometimes necessitated splitting them into halves or thirds.

Willow and other twigs used as round rods may be peeled or left with the bark on. Boiling or soaking may be needed to soften the bark. Some barks may simply be stripped off with a knife or the teeth—that is, the twig clamped between the teeth and pulled out of the bark—followed by scraping to remove the bumps. The smoothing is commonly done with a knife, but Cherokee weavers smooth and polish honeysuckle vine by rubbing it with handfuls of sand; some Hopi use a piece of sandstone to rub irregularities off peeled rabbit brush or sumac rods. Many American Indians have relied on their teeth as a handy tool for stripping bark or splitting; the Chitimacha prepare cane this way even today. The shiny outer surface of the cane, the part used, is peeled (removed) with the teeth from split lengths.

German immigrants also made the well-known coiled baskets of rye straw, although wheat and other straws could be and were employed. The straw, rather than being a waste product from the threshing floor thriftily put to good purpose, has to be perfect, not bruised or bent, unthreshed straw. Rye straw has been preferred for its length and toughness.

The only coiling tool is an awl or needle, used to make an opening in or around the preceding coil(s), through which the binding fiber or thread is pushed or carried. Before they acquired metal implements through trade, Indians made a simple awl of a solid bone from a deer's leg, a cactus thorn, or a sharpened piece of wood.

CONSTRUCTION

The ubiquitous American basket is the *rib-type*, a basket of countless names: melon or gizzard (for its shape), pack, saddle, or bow (Cherokee), hip (Southern Highlands), buttocks (English translation of the Pennsylvania Dutch for its bulging resemblance to the human seat), as well as earthier or cute ones like "Granny's fanny," which any number of families believe they have coined. Figure 5 illustrates the construction, which starts with a continuous handle being bound to a rim hoop at right angles. Curving ribs are inserted into the two joints to form a heavy skeleton resembling a rib cage. Examination of plate 61 shows the various shapes: round, oval, or rectangular, with the bottom either rounded (a few oval ones have a stabilizing flattened extension of the all-around handle out to the side), nearly flat in the rectangular form, or "splitting." The separation facilitated balancing the basket on a hip or across the neck of a horse or mule in front of the rider. Although it is true that most baskets do have ribs, I prefer the term *rib-basket* because the ribs are the most prominent physical aspect and unifying characteristic of these baskets; it serves as an umbrella to cover the whole range of variations on a theme to be found sharing this construction. When I need to describe a rib-basket, I have found that a good way to put it is that "curving ribs seem to radiate from the handle ends." (Plates 63 and 64 show two unusual baskets based on the construction.)

Although rib-type construction must be dispersed throughout the

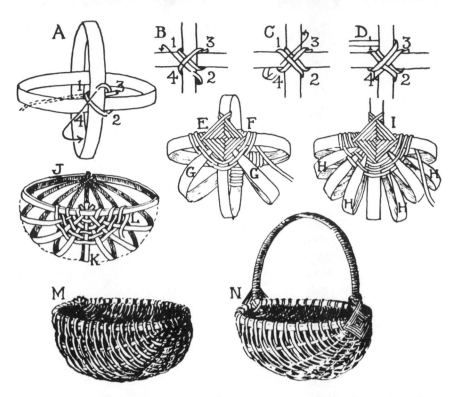

FIGURE 5. Construction of rib-type basket. Begun with two hoops bound at right angles to become the rim and handle, which goes all around. Each rib is securely held in two wrapped joints, here employing the "folded square." The drawings are self-explanatory when studied by letter progression and numbers; J and M illustrate the handle-free version. Bottoms may be quite rounded, nearly flat, or "splitting," that is, separating to result in two curving sections. The construction is employed in other forms. This is the ubiquitous American basket, based on European antecedents and known by many names: melon or gizzard (for its shape), hip (Southern Highlands), buttocks (a translation of the Pennsylvania German, for its bulging resemblance to the human seat), pack, saddle, or bow (Cherokee), and countless others. Illustrations courtesy Osma Gallinger Tod.

world—new examples are coming from such far-flung sources as Sweden, the Orient, and South Africa—it sailed to these shores from Europe, being especially prevalent in the British Isles. In fact, the ancient Britons were celebrated as early as Roman times for their basketry skills; great quantities of their baskets were imported into Rome, where they figured among the most esteemed and expensive table trappings.[6]

The Cherokee quickly adopted the sturdy rib-type design from whites arriving in their misty mountains, so that it has sometimes been thought of and referred to, inaccurately, as a traditional Cherokee type. Actually, basketweaving techniques and forms were exchanged among the immigrants and the natives, often through intermarriage. The April 1973 issue of *The Ozarks Mountaineer* [7] featured Clarence Baggett, a fourth-generation white oak rib-basket weaver of Grandin, Missouri, whose grandfather learned from his North Carolina Cherokee mother. It was said that a basket made by the latter gentleman was still strong enough to carry a peck of rocks after fifty years of use.

A basketmaker's work procedure may call for completing each basket as an entirely individual unit, or, in the case of simpler plaited splintwork, producing a group of twenty or more taken together from step to step. The bottom of a basket is made first. The simplest splint construction is that with a square bottom; the rib-type is more difficult. In the former, the elements are interwoven lying on a flat surface, one practice being to lay it out on the floor to fit a pattern marked with chalk. In basketry, a complete movement is called a *stroke*. After the bottom is ready, the splints are bent up at the sides to function as the warp elements or uprights called *ribs, stakes,* or *standards* in some locales. (However, Nantucket Lightship Basket weavers use sailors' coopering terms and, for example, call their uprights *staves*.) It may be necessary to split one rib to get an uneven number in order to make the weaving pattern. The weft (woof) or horizontal elements, called *weavers, fillers,* or *fills,* are passed over and under the ribs.

A *course* is a complete circumference of the basket with a weaver. When a weaver runs out, it is *pieced* by introducing a new one, taking a generous overlap, and keeping the ends inside the basket (tucking them under so that they won't protrude). After the basket is deep enough, it is set aside to dry, for a few hours or as long as three weeks. The shrinkage is then *pulled down,* that is, the weavers are pushed downward as close together as possible to get a tight basket. Northeastern Indian weavers cut off every other rib but turned (bent) the others back over the top weaver, trimmed them to points, and tucked them under a lower weaver. The procedure is called *hemming* and results in firming the *edge* or *lip*. The rim hoop is bound on with a flexible strip called the *binding,* the *lashing,* or the *lacer,* with the procedure usually known as *binding* but in some localities called *sewing* or *tying.* With a double-rim basket, one hoop is inside and the other goes around the outside of the edge and handle, if there is one.

Splints have been termed *basket stuff* in New England, but are called *splits* in the Appalachians and the Ozarks, where a basket of white oak splint may be referred to as a split-oak basket or as an oak-split basket. *The Foxfire Book* (1972) contains a series of closeup photographs of a simple, square-bottomed cotton hamper in construction and a set of instructive shots for a rib-basket as well.

A square-bottomed splint basket may be given a round mouth with the addition of a strong *hoop* or *rim* bound into that shape, as was the example in plate 28. The Eastern Band of Cherokee make a complex square-to-round cuplike burden basket with a deep, square bottom and bowl-shaped upper portion (pl. 18).

A round-bottomed basket is more difficult to weave than one with a squared bottom, and an oval shape more difficult still, although using a wooden base makes the job easier. In the latter method, the sides are constructed and then a wooden base fitted inside; the two are attached by hammering nails through a wooden band around the outside. Another method, illustrated in Nantucket Lightship Baskets, is to force the ribs into a groove sawed all around the wooden base just inside the edge. In the wood-bottomed basket in plate 23, the groove runs all along the side of the base, the ribs are deeply inserted, and a half-dozen nails are hammered in for durability.

The structure of a woven round *base* (bottom) reminds one of a spider web, and is sometimes so called, in that *spokes* go through the center (one is split to get an uneven number), and a weaver passes under and over them until the selected diameter is reached. The spokes are then pulled in as the weaver continues around, so that they become the uprights.

It is desirable to have a domed base, that is, a high center, to carry part of the weight to the outside of the basket, where it is stronger, and to avoid crushing or bruising fragile contents. The basket in plate 69 has a five-inch-high raised center, and the Michigan apple basket of plate 68 has what is also called an "inverted demijohn" bottom. A splint basket with a dome-shaped bottom can be started on top of a wooden mold made of a set of stepped concentric circles or on a half globe. The Colonial Williamsburg weavers simply weave flat-bottomed round baskets and then punch them in with the fist.

Various ways have been devised to hold the basket steady, such as impaling the bottom on a spike in the workbench, thus freeing both hands to work. Many weavers hold them in their laps with their knees, some just hang the started basket upside down on a post. An old drawing shows an Iroquois woman weaving a round splint basket while it is suspended upside down from a tree branch by a cord through the bottom, a device known to other Amerinds.

The most loosely used word in the basketry vocabulary has to be *wicker*. I have seen it employed to describe: (1) plaited hexagonal openwork baskets in a farm museum's exhibit on cheesemaking; (2) a wide variety of imported baskets, including coiled ones, in a department store's full-page housewares advertisement; and (3) baskets in general, in a leading home magazine's enthusiastic text about the country look in decorating. There is precedent enough for confusion, and my examination of unabridged dictionaries has failed to provide clarification. For the purpose of this book, *wicker* will be used in only two senses: (1) as a noun, meaning wickerwork or wicker weave, and (2) as an adjective, for a basket woven by that technique.

By far, the most common material used in wickerwork is willow; weavers are called *rods* when in-the-round, or *osiers,* which is the name for any of various willows with tough, flexible twigs that are used in basketry. Willow rods may be split into *strips* for fine weaving.

FIGURE 6. The Basketmaker, 1823. These drawings appeared on the same page with depictions of coopering in what must have been a volume on trades. The man with the hat (bottom row), having completed a spider-web base, is tying in the uprights to facilitate weaving the fairly straight sides of a tall basket; the other craftsman is filling in an oval basket. Photograph courtesy the Smithsonian Institution, Washington, D.C.

Although willow wood occasionally appears in splint baskets (pl. 66), the term *willow basket* commonly describes a wicker basket of willow rods. A round and an oval wicker basket are shown in construction in figure 6, which is taken from the "Basket Makers and Coopers" section of an 1823 volume on trades.

Various borders may be applied to the rim of a wicker basket. Splint baskets (other than some with a nailed rim) have a *wrapped border, single-* or *double-bound,* the latter also known as *cross-bound* or *X-bound.* A border around the outside of the bottom is a *base border,* which strengthens the basket and makes future replacement possible when worn, so that the basket may be returned to active duty. This frugal detail was a trademark of the willow baskets of the Amana Colonies of Iowa (pl. 73).

Basketmakers and fanciers consider the *rake* of the sides a point of beauty. This refers to the inclination from the vertical or horizontal —the flare or slope, curve or swell.

Handles may be of splint, a smoothed or natural withe, carved wood, or a group of twisted twigs or stems. They may be rigid or movable. A carved handle is notched to fit around the inside hoop of a double rim. Each end of a rigid handle is inserted between the weavers and the ribs and is bound on. Rigid handles may run the length of the basket, rather than crossing the width (usual). Movable or flexible handles—it is common to find a pair of swing, or drop, handles on a shopper—may be attached with carved wood fittings bound to the outside or inside of the basket, loops tied in, or with an ear-and-pin device. Rather than a central handle, there may be a small pair opposite each other (or even three, which is rare) or openings under the rim as handholds or grips (see the two baskets at the left in pl. 61). Plate 2 shows a basket in which the movable handle has been pinned by pegs to wedge-shaped sockets, as in old wooden buckets. The photographs in this volume show the range of possibilities in combination with other features. Plate 38 shows a handle that has been carved to resemble lathe-turned work.

Covers or lids may be attached with loops or binding strips, slotted to slide up on the rigid handle rather than lifting off (feather-type, as in pl. 34), or, on lunch baskets, come in two sections—connected to the ends to open outward or to a bar running across the rim under the handle to open upward.

The *foundation* of a coiled basket may consist of a group of rods, or a bundle of, say, grasses, or a combination of a bundle and rods. One starts the basket with a knot of the foundation fiber or by wrapping a short portion of the *bundle* of *core material* with a flexible *binding strip* (*lashing*, also called a *thread* or *sewing strand*), then bending it into a loop and stitching it down flat. The basket is *sewn* or *stitched* with the aid of an awl or needle as the binding is passed over the top coil and pushed or pulled through (or around) the coil(s) below, and the work proceeds in a continuous spiral. Addi-

FIGURE 7. Hopi artisan (Hazel Yuyaheova) coiling plaque/tray characteristic of Second Mesa, Arizona. Foundation consists of bundles of grass or yucca, sewn with split yucca-leaf binding. The Hopi use both homemade and commercial dyes. Photograph courtesy *House Beautiful*, copyright © 1971 by the Hearst Corporation.

tional core material is worked in as needed. A Second Mesa, Arizona, Hopi craftswoman demonstrates coiling in figure 7.

The center (beginning) coils are usually a little smaller in circumference, and better baskets tend to be of thinner coils. The foundation material may be left mostly exposed or be completely covered over with binding, in which case finer quality baskets have more stitches per square inch. Amerinds typically coil in a counterclockwise direction, whereas Afro-Americans and whites usually produce a clockwise spiral. Crafts books advise working in whichever direction seems easier, and the advice is so logical that some weavers must have decided on their own to defy tradition.

Southern Paiute and Ute basketmakers, whose basketry was built clockwise, changed to counterclockwise to suit the strictly prescribed requirements for wedding baskets of Navajo customers who had moved into the lands around them about 1860 and had pretty much dropped basketry in favor of the more profitable textile weaving and to avoid the numerous restrictions attendant upon the maker during the manufacture of a ceremonial basket. The suppliers also had to accommodate by copying a shape and design different from theirs and even to change the method of sewing.[8]

FUNCTION

A farm was a many-faceted operation involving grain crops, poultry, and dairying, and a spread of other activities, including orchardry and home canning. While she bore and cared for the children, the hard-working farm woman made and mended most of the clothes and bedding, did the laundry and cooking, and tended a kitchen garden of vegetables and herbs and probably the chickens, besides. What must have been the endless labors of Colonial and pioneer household, farmyard, and field required any number of baskets, some multipurpose and others tailored to a unique application. The name *chore-basket* has sometimes been applied to a multiuse form of personal or local preference.

A basket's planned function determines its size and need for strength. Intended service influences selection of material and weave, although it often happens that a form can be and is found in both plaited splint and wickerwork.

Two prime examples of special-purpose basketry are the weaving of fiber covering right over glass bottles to protect them from breakage in shipping or everyday handling (fig. 8) and baskets made in exact sizes to be used as measures, as was a round splint *collier's basket* that held two bushels of charcoal. *Nesting sets* (a small-sized new one appears in pl. 41) saved space.

What is an *egg basket?* A handled basket taken on the daily round of egg collecting—usually a rib-type in the Southern Highlands

FIGURE 8. Basketry-covered bottle. From New York State, of a wicker weave often used for the purpose throughout the Northeast up to the end of the 1800s. (One historical reference mentions local Indians who were employed in a factory producing basketry-encased bottles.) The woven-on (wet) fiber sheath—usually of willow but sometimes oak-splint—protected the handblown glass from breakage in shipment or handling; the handle, cheaper and safer to build into the covering, facilitated carrying the quart bottle back and forth to refill its whiskey, wine, or brandy contents. This glass is amber colored, any tint being rarer than the usual clear. Larger bottles were for vinegar. Sometimes-huge demijohns that brought alcoholic beverages from Europe and the West Indies are common along the Eastern Seaboard. H. 10¼"; Diam. 4¼".

and a round splint in New England—and used in between for carrying all kinds of things. One version of a Kentucky egg basket (pl. 64) had long, flattened sides so that it would lie flat against the horse or mule's body as it hung from the saddle pommel; some of them were reputed to have been woven to hold exact dozens of eggs.

FIELD AND ORCHARD. Research into *potato baskets* uncovered two writers who offered differing descriptions, one resembling those deep ones in figure 9 and the other supposed to be round-bottomed bushels convenient to drag along the rows. Even though "shod with heavy strips of splints," it is difficult to imagine how the latter could have survived long, being pulled across rough ground with that heavy load resting smack on the middle of that rounded bottom. Yet another potato basket is included in plate 14; it is used to hand-gather machine-dug potatoes in Aroostook County, northern Maine.

An *apple basket* might look like the heavyweight Michigan splint in plate 68 or the Amana wicker in figure 10. *Picking baskets* had a loop or pair of handles at the rim so they could be suspended from a cord about the waist. One researcher found a fruit-gathering basket of flattened form in rib-type construction that suspended from a dowel and slung from a cord over the picker's shoulder as he climbed up into an apple tree. A *peach basket* had flaring sides that helped support

FIGURE 9. Digging potatoes by hand on a truck farm on Long Island, New York: date uncertain. Photograph courtesy the Smithsonian Institution, Washington, D.C.

the weight, to avoid bruising the fruits at the bottom. However, the peach basket known to the expert Hopi farmer was a crude wicker-work affair with U-shaped corner supports (other Southwest and Prairie tribes had them as well). Peaches, grown from the descendants of trees sent as a gift to the Hopi from Queen Isabella of Spain, have been a valuable crop, the bulk of which is dried for food and sale.

One kind of field basket is of the "bushel" type, used for gathering heavy produce like root and head vegetables. An Amana Colonies version is included in plate 73. The most common basket in Texas was a product of the cotton culture; the *cotton basket* is a square-bottomed (often round-bottom elsewhere) white oak- or ash-splint with a round, wide mouth and grip openings under the rim that was found on all southern farms in the nineteenth century. Placed at the ends of the rows, the pickers emptied their sacks into it, to be carried to the

FIGURE 10. Boys dismissed from class to pick fruit, Amana Colonies of Iowa: 1910–1920. The Amanas were established by a communal sect that practiced extensive agriculture and conducted several small industries. Sturdy wickerwork baskets of willow were made in quantity for their own use. Although not clear in the photo, fruit-gathering baskets often had a pair of handles close together at the rim, so that they could be suspended from the waist with a belt or cord. Photograph courtesy Joan Liffring Zug.

wagon. I have heard this basket called a *corn basket* in the Southern Highlands and the Ozarks, and it looks like what a gardener knows as a *yard/litter/leaf basket*. (Sears's version from the end of the century had a pair of handles and was touted as being multipurpose.) A smaller-sized cotton basket, about a foot high with an eighteen-inch mouth, is known in Texas as a *shuck basket* and carried corn shucks for mule feed.

The rarely seen *seed baskets* were double-woven. *Sowing baskets* came in several forms. One was round, several inches deep, and had three handles at the rim, two to slip a rope through to tie around the waist and the third for a hand, to steady it against the body. It was of coiled straw among the Pennsylvania Germans, splint elsewhere. An unusual fan-shaped splint Southern Appalachian sowing basket, intended to rest against the hip, is included in figure 11. Another splint was a kind of vase shape, into which the hand could be thrust.

FARM INDUSTRIES. Separating the grain from the straw and chaff called for: a *riddle,* a shallow, round basket (often basketry attached to a wooden frame) with large square holes in the bottom for separating out the heavy straws; after flailing, a *winnowing fan* (pl. 1) to scoop up the grain, which was tossed into the air, the wind carrying away the light, empty hulls while the kernels fell back into the basket or were dropped to the threshing floor or into another basket; and *sieves.* The latter were also used to clean or sort beans and small fruits and vegetables by size.

A very long, rigid-handled, oval plaited splint basket has been identified by an antiques dealer as a grain basket; he had come across an illustration in an old book that depicted such a basket filled with grain on the stalk. It would have been fine for carrying in the rye straw for coiled baskets, because the weaver must start with whole, unbroken stems. Of course, grain had to be stored in baskets, too. The Pimas of the Southwest coiled huge, round granary baskets as they sat inside them.

Cheese curd baskets or *cheese baskets* (pl. 32) are sometimes called *cheese drainers,* or, less accurately, *cheese sieves.* They are usually of hexagonal openwork splint, although a handled version with square-holed openwork bottom and solid woven sides is shown in Mary Earle Gould's *Early American Wooden Ware & Other Wooden Utensils* (1942). Cheese baskets were lined with cloth, filled with the curd mass, and set on racks over vats to catch the dripping whey. Small hexagonal openwork splint baskets are found and called cheese baskets, too, although most were used for kitchen storage and other purposes, as they were among the Shakers (pl. 45). Cheese baskets were still in common use after the Civil War, but not after cheese factories became established toward the century's close.

HOUSEHOLD. An incredible variety of tasks were performed by the diligent women of the household. Baskets for drying fruit or draining wet wash or rinsing wool had large-openwork bottoms. *Fruit-drying baskets* were good-sized shallow trays, sometimes set on the windowsill so half could be sunning outside. *Laundry/wash baskets* had a pair of handles at the rim and might be square-bottomed-to-round-mouthed (pl. 3) or oval-mouthed in the case of Indian-made splint examples produced for sale. A *wool-rinsing basket* was supposed to have been set up on legs so that it could be rested on the bottom of a running stream (pl. 4). The only other four-legged basket I have examined was a large, closely woven, sturdily reinforced rectangular

FIGURE 11. Temporary basketry exhibit at the Smithsonian Institution: August–September 1973. From the collection of the Division of Textiles. The fan-shaped splint basket (lower center) is a North Carolina seed-grain sowing basket—the curve of the hickory frame is held against the hip with a hand out on the handle. The three-handled wickerwork jardiniere from Kentucky (lower right) is of unpeeled willow. Both would have been made during the period of the crafts revival, which was notably successful in the Southern Appalachian Highlands, earlier in the century. Photograph courtesy the Smithsonian Institution, Washington, D.C.

ash-splint with solid bottom. Its intended use is unknown, but one might speculate that the legs were needed to keep some obviously heavy contents up off a damp floor.

A rectangular splint *bed basket (baby basket)*, part of the top of which is removable, is illustrated in *American Basketry and Woodenware* (1974) by William C. Ketchum, Jr. There were cradles of basketry, and one researcher encountered an oval rib-basket with a round bottom that was reputed to have been so used.

Spinning and weaving were once common household tasks, and a loom room had: *storage hampers* (pl. 44); *bobbin baskets,* wall-hung and of splint, with a stepped backplate; and perhaps slender, handled *flax baskets. Sewing/work/mending/darning baskets* were round, often with covers and sometimes handles. Plate 5 shows two uncovered versions, now often thought of as *table baskets for fruit.* Those of open-work would have been lined when holding small needlework objects that might fall through.

Geese have nasty tempers and object most strenuously to the usual live plucking. To avoid being bitten, the plucker covered the bird's head with a stocking or wedged it upside down into a *goose basket.* This was ovoid or egg-shaped, often without handles, and deep enough to contain the longnecked bird's head and shoulders. It could be used to store the goose down or feathers. The name is being applied to large examples that were probably made for and used as clothes hampers (pls. 29 and 70).

A so-called *feather basket* is a different thing (pl. 34). The cover does not come off but slides up on the handle so that it may be raised with the side of the plucker's hand as she stuffs the fistful of snatched feathers into it. The other hand would be occupied with the struggling bird, and the feathers would blow away if not confined. Most feather-type examples are really too small to have been practical for that, but the form is not uncommon and must have been popular. Some saw service as knitting baskets.

A Pennsylvania German *bread-raising/dough basket* of coiled straw held the shaped loaves while they rose overnight before being baked (pl. 51). Everywhere, baskets were needed to carry food to school, field, church, or social events. Two probable individual lunch baskets are shown in plate 6. Plate 7 includes a large covered oval with two swing handles that is often referred to as an Amish or Mennonite family lunch basket. The type does indeed appear in photographs with them, but I'm told that this basket would once have been considered too "fancy" by these strict people. Other picnic hampers are shown in plates 17 and 62. Plate 40 includes a recent New Hampshire *pie basket,* plate 14 a new *double pie basket* by a weaver of Passamaquoddy heritage, and new Arkansas Ozarks food carriers are included in plate 74.

A *market basket* or *shopper* (pl. 8) is a handled basket that doubled as a gathering basket for the home vegetable garden. It took butter and eggs to market and brought back salt, sugar, coffee, flour, and a few other purchased necessaries. A handled Algonkian *berry-picking basket* is shown in plate 12, but other square-lined berry baskets had no handles. They tended to have tightly woven bottoms, to prevent the berries below from being squashed into openings.

A *flower/cutting basket* (pl. 9) brought the blooms to the house; the form is known as a *sandwich basket* in Arkansas. A *wall basket* is any basket made to be hung on the wall, and it may be a *half-basket,* that is, literally half of a round rib-type enclosed with a vertical, flat side; the term *wall pocket* has been applied to some Indian-made types.

Both *wood/log/chip/kindling baskets* (used nowadays as magazine baskets) and *wastebaskets* were late arrivals on the American scene. In Colonial times, wood was stacked conveniently near the fireplace. There are three common wood-basket forms; two are shown in plate 10, and the other has rectangular sides. One heavy, practical working piece examined was eighteen inches long by fifteen inches wide and seventeen inches high with handle, its ends bound with metal strap instead of splint. Wastebaskets have taken various forms and proved necessary once paper became so cheap, and paperwork so plentiful, that it could be thrown away with impunity (and fireplaces had ceased to burn continuously). They began to appear in American schools and offices in the mid-nineteenth century, then almost always as wicker with openwork sides.

HUNTING AND FISHING. Although trapping was mostly undertaken by professionals, it was a highly profitable, if strenuous, part-time occupation for a lot of farmers. A *trapper's basket* was a *pack basket;* this has a flattened rear so it can be worn against the back. It is supported by straps that pass over the shoulders and under the arms. A very special basket was a *pigeon carrier* or *basket* (pl. 25) for transporting wild passenger pigeons as decoys for netting or for target practice.

A *fisherman's scale basket,* long made by the Passamaquoddy of Maine, is included in plate 14. For many generations, the tribe has been known for its fishing skills and the manufacture of utility baskets that give rugged service while subjected to constant soaking and drying out. Large, handled baskets with openwork bottoms unloaded the catch of the Eastern Seaboard, and *clam and oyster baskets* came in measure sizes.

The well-recognized *fishing creel* or *trout basket* has its counterpart in the Cherokee fish basket of plate 18, which would hang at one's side from a thong across the chest and was purposely made small to remind the angler to catch no more than needed.

OTHER. Gift baskets included Easter baskets and small ones to please children. The weaving of miniature baskets (pl. 11) has been undertaken, by Indians particularly, as a pleasurable show of skill.

Church collection baskets were round baskets attached to long wooden handles. A *liebesbrot* or *communion-bread basket* from the Amana Colonies of Iowa is shown in plate 73.

Trade baskets is more a British term to describe those made for some ·special occupation or aspect of commerce, often connected with the delivery of products. Such baskets were strictly utilitarian, as was the twenty-eight-inch-long basket in plate 71, which was used very early in this century in Chicago for wholesale meat delivery. Larger examples had a pair of handles at the ends so that two men could carry a hundred pounds.

To name several other forms basketry has taken, there were eel and fish traps, ox muzzles, funnels, and coiled-straw *skeps* or beehives. This book could not accommodate all the possibilities.

No machine has been invented that can weave baskets. In preceding centuries, they were the most common containers. But the industrial revolution, mechanized farming, and machine-made patented stave baskets, which came into wide use toward the end of the nineteenth century, followed by mass-produced paper, glass, metal, and plastic containers, virtually eliminated the practical need for hand-woven baskets.

They were not simply replaced, but agricultural machinery, including complex, integrated harvesting and bulk commodity-handling systems, took over activities that had previously required quantities of human labor using baskets. The transition from a heavily rural culture to a preponderantly urban culture left behind the function of many household baskets, too, and those of us who live with hand-woven baskets today do so primarily because it is our pleasure.

DECORATION

Norman Feder writes in *Two Hundred Years of North American Indian Art* (1971): ". . . Indians tended to decorate almost everything they used, as time and materials allowed. The motivations for decoration were not unique to American Indians, including as they do the desire for prestige, vanity, pride in craftsmanship, and the giving of gifts to loved ones."[9] However, baskets for short-term use and some working baskets were perfectly plain.

PATTERN. Pattern may be achieved through weave. The plaiting technique of twill, in which each new row is started one warp to the right or left, results in a diagonal pattern. A herringbone or zigzag results from alternating the diagonal movement from side to side.

The Cherokee of North Carolina employ these patterns in their river-cane and white-oak splintwork, and twilled square bottoms are common in the Arkansas Ozarks.

Indian women did not have written or drawn patterns of any kind, but created the surface and the design simultaneously (they count stitches), as in the beautiful twined or coiled baskets for which the Pomo and other western tribes were noted. (Another West Coast tribe painted onto the exterior of coiled baskets designs that could have been woven in.) The application of the geometric motifs of the swastika, maze, and frets by Indians of the American Southwest arose independently, long before white contact, and cannot be linked with their common use in Greek, Cretan, and other European artifacts.

Interest may be gained by employing two weaves and/or materials. The Hopi *piki* tray of plate 22 is of plaited split sumac and round-rod sumac wickerwork.

A practice common among Eastern Woodlands Indians is to vary the width of splint weavers. Leaving openings between them permits a pattern of light to fall through the spaces. The effect of the openwork in the familiar willow or honeysuckle vine sewing baskets and the hexagonal openwork usual in cheese baskets also render them pleasing to the eye.

COLOR. Color may be supplied by the materials themselves. The design in Hopi yucca-leaf sifters (pl. 22) is made visible with green (outer), yellow (sun-bleached), and white (core) leaves. Dead pine needles are reddish brown, whereas those picked when fresh remain greenish. White oak heartwood is darker than the sapwood and so may be used for a decorative band. Peeled or unpeeled willow rods or those cut at different times of the year offer color variation. In the Amana market basket in plate 73, alternating peeled and unpeeled osiers and passing all osiers of each kind over and under the same ribs result in a pattern of vertical dark and light bands, identical to that seen in a new French herring basket. If, instead of alternating, the peeled and unpeeled osiers—or rods or splints in two colors—are layered, a checkerboard design results.

Obviously, plant materials available for dyes vary with the region. The Cherokee of North Carolina use mostly roots (but also some walnut hulls and even green walnut leaves, the latter for a light green). Barks, seeds, stems, twigs, berries, flowers, saps or juices, and some animal or mineral substances such as wood ash and clays have been used elsewhere, often in combinations. Brewing one's own stains from collected materials presumes access to plant sources and knowledge of the processes, including mordants (color fixatives), as well as the expenditure of a great deal of time and effort. Among the Hopi, some weavers make a point of preparing all their own natural stains, while others use both native and synthetic formulas. Vegetal colors give softer shades that resist fading; bright aniline dyes weaken quickly and mellow appreciably or fade out with time. They were developed at the end of the nineteenth century to replace the difficult-to-control indigo (a leading natural plant dyestuff that very early proved popular among Indian customers of white traders) and named from the Arabic word *anil* for it. It is common for weavers of Indian heritage in the Northeast to obtain their synthetic colors by leaching them from crepe paper.

The normal procedure is to soak the splints in dye pots, although pigmentation is occasionally found, instead, to have been painted on one side before weaving. Color has also been added with simple floral or geometric freehand-painted or potato-type design stampings of leaves, dots, suns, feathers, etc., applied to wide weavers with berry juices or other plant stains. There appears to be no spiritual significance to the motifs or symbols. Such decorative effects could easily have been accomplished by non-Indian weavers but probably seldom were.

The whole basket may be colored, as was the Michigan apple basket in plate 68, probably originally, with sumac stain. Enough nineteenth-century baskets were painted in dark forest green, blue green, blue, red, pumpkin, black, brown, or white, in the same homemade paints as on furniture and buildings of the period, that some collectors are specializing in them. These paints had a buttermilk or egg-white binder and might employ as pigment anything from the green corrosion scraped off copper to mashed berries, colored clay, and even soot.

ORNAMENTATION. As they exploited their environment for varied plant materials, so American Indians exploited the weaver's latitude in stylistic aspects. The Pomo, the only Amerinds to produce baskets using all techniques, expertly incorporated shimmering feathers, by working them onto the surface of coiled, enclosed-bowl shapes, and they and other tribes sometimes added such elements as shells and beads to beautiful ceremonial and gift baskets. The conical Apache burden basket had buckskin fringe and numerous bells attached at the ends of leather strips; the pleasant tinkling as the bearers moved about was called "women's music."

Algonkian and Iroquoian tribes and others of the Great Lakes use an interesting technique for decorating splint baskets that was introduced around 1860. It involves a twisted overlay strip called *curlicue* (*curly* to present-day Passamaquoddy and Penobscot weavers of Maine), *roll,* or *porcupine,* the strips being brought out into curls or projecting points (pls. 15 and 16).

Imbrication is a method of ornamentation superimposed on coiled baskets, used by tribes of the Pacific Northwest, in which colored fiber strips are added by nipping them in on the exterior surface only. It differs from *false embroidery* in that flat ribbons rather than strands are used. Iroquois false embroidery of dyed moose hair once decorated basketry *tumplines,* flat straps that pass over the forehead and attach to or are used in connection with carrying baskets.

On openwork border may be added onto coiled baskets by pulling out and binding the outside coil(s) away from the construction, as in a Pennsylvania German example included in plate 52 and in some Gullah baskets. Strictly decorative, also, are the vertical outside spokes on the Amana *liebesbrot* basket of plate 73.

NOTES

1. Frank G. Speck, "Decorative Art and Basketry of the Cherokee," *Bulletin of the Public Museum of the City of Milwaukee,* Vol. 2, No. 2 (Milwaukee, Wisc.: July 27, 1920).
2. John M. Goggin, "Plaited Basketry in the New World," *Southwestern*

Journal of Anthropology, Vol. 5 (Albuquerque, N.M.: University of New Mexico Press, 1949).

3. Jan Hobbs, "Basket study moves to Unity," *Bangor* (Maine) *Daily News,* February 20, 1974. The Canadian interviewee, Miss Gaby Pelletier, mentioned a "well-based study done by Ted Brasser . . . curator of the ethnology department at the Museum of Man and Nature in Ottawa."

4. Frank G. Speck, *Eastern Algonkian Block-Stamp Decoration: A New World Original or an Acculturated Art,* Research Series No. 1 (Trenton, N.J.: The Archeological Society of New Jersey, The State Museum, 1947).

5. Volney H. Jones, "Some Chippewa and Ottawa Uses of Sweet Grass," *Papers of the Michigan Academy of Science, Arts and Letters,* Vol. 21 (Ann Arbor, Mich.: University of Michigan Press, 1936).

6. Thomas Martin, *The New Circle of the Mechanical Arts* (London: for J. Bumpus, 1819), p. 62.

7. Joyce L. Porterfield, "Last of the Basketmaking Baggetts," *The Ozarks Mountaineer* (April 1973).

8. Omer C. Stewart, "The Navajo Wedding Basket—1938," *Museum Notes,* Vol. 10, No. 9 (Flagstaff, Ariz.: Museum of Northern Arizona, March 1938).

9. Norman Feder, *Two Hundred Years of North American Indian Art* (New York: Praeger Publishers, Inc., in association with the Whitney Museum of American Art, 1971).

3.

Ethnic, Communal, and Regional Origins

AMERICAN INDIAN

The Pilgrim fathers and mothers might not have survived that first American winter without the find of a goodly cache of corn in large, round storage baskets buried in the sand. European explorers were amazed to see fiber basketry "substituting" for metal and other materials that they took for granted. Among American Indians, basketry items included an incredible array of objects, from seed beaters to armor, in addition to those for the mundane transport, storage, and food preparation functions of daily living. Some baskets were so tightly woven that they would hold liquids, and mush was cooked by throwing hot stones into a basket filled with water and ground grain or nuts. Its sides would be supported by placement in a hollowed-out spot in the sand or soil. The Papago of the Southwest ceremonially drank *tiswin* (a syrupy liquor of low alcoholic content fermented from the boiled ripe fruit of the saguaro cactus) from special baskets.

Although, among groups relying mainly on leather, birchbark, or pottery, basketry was a lesser craft, necessity made it the major craft for numerous tribes. A family might own a dozen or more baskets suited to its various needs. The Indians had no indigenous beast of burden, other than the dogs held by some, and relied upon pack baskets balanced on their own shoulders, often by means of a tumpline across the forehead that passed low around the spreading conical form to which these baskets tend.

Here is a brief survey of Amerindian baskets by region, with the emphasis on living forms:

The *Northeast* includes the Algonkin (Algonquin)-speaking and Iroquoian tribes, producers of ash-splint baskets. Sweet grass, a favorite among the Indians themselves, is woven over splint ribs to make round, covered sewing or trinket baskets by Iroquois of New York, the Penobscots on Indian Island, Old Town, Maine, and the Passamaquoddy of Washington County, Maine (located at Pleasant Point in Perry and Peter Dana Point, Indian Township, near Princeton), as well as by some tribes of the western Great Lakes. The Passamaquoddy weave quantities of sturdy, undecorated black ash-splint utility baskets, including pack baskets, which are much in evidence in stores in Maine. Their decorated baskets are a more recent development. It is evident from the appearance of basket co-ops at both reservations, with a retail outlet maintained at Calais and the possible opening of stores in Bangor and Bar Harbor, that basketry is beginning to afford the Passamaquoddy a practicable livelihood. Plate 14 shows new ash-splint utility baskets by Algonkian weavers of Maine and plate 15 decorated baskets from Northeastern tribes.

It is often difficult to distinguish among the new splintwork of New England Algonkian and New York Iroquoian tribes or that of others farther west, such as the (Siouan) Winnebagos and Menomini (Menominees) of Wisconsin and the Ottawas and Chippewas of Michigan. The groups all use ash splint, do ornamental curlicue work, employ synthetic dyes, and most forms are made for sale.

Formerly, the Mahicans and other Algonkians and some Iroquois cut simple designs into sections of raw potato, turnip, wood, or other material soft enough to be carved, then dipped the block-stamp into berry juice and other plant dyes and applied it to broad weavers (pl. 13). Algonkians had previously freehand painted on dots and casual patterns (pl. 12). Neither technique survives today, although potato-stamping appears in non-Indian schoolcraft projects.

Algonkians arrived in Ohio when they were pushed from their lands along the Eastern Seaboard. They must have been prolific basketweavers earlier this century, judging from the numbers of their splint baskets that are encountered in that state (see pl. 16 showing baskets from the western Great Lakes region), but Ohio Historical Society curators know of no Indian basketmaking today. There are also plenty of early twentieth-century Indian-made splint baskets in Michigan and Wisconsin, where they were sold from roadside stands. Western Great Lakes tribes, including, until recently, the Woodland Ojibwa (Chippewa) of Minnesota, have produced wickerwork of willow.

In the *Southeast* the Eastern Band of Cherokee in North Carolina (part of the Iroquoian linguistic group) weave quantities of well-made baskets of white oak splint, river cane, or honeysuckle vine (pl. 18). Cherokee weavers usually prefer to concentrate on one of the three fibers and brew their own plant dyes. Diamond patterns predominate in river-cane plaiting, and, when these designs are executed in white oak splint, the pattern is referred to as *river-cane weave*. *Doubleweave*, which was nearly lost, was revived in the 1940s with the aid of an "ancient of the tribe" and a photograph of a specimen that had been in the British Museum since 1725.[1] This complex technique consists of weaving one river-cane basket inside another in one continuous weave and results in a different pattern inside and out; the elements are "worked up" the sides obliquely, rather than at right angles to each other. The Oklahoma Cherokees, who were forcibly removed from North Carolina in the late 1830s, weave baskets of modern design from buckbrush runners and employ commercial dyes.

Plate 19 shows three baskets attributed to Southern Woodlands tribes. Some coiled sweet-grass basketry is made by the Seminoles of Florida. A few among the Eastern Band of Choctaws at Philadelphia, Mississippi, do plaited swamp-cane weaving, including a revived doubleweave. A number of (approximately sixty) Coushatta (Koasati) at Elton, Louisiana, coil longleaf pine-needle or sedge-grass baskets and plait swamp cane and some white oak. The Alabama-Coushatta Reservation near Livingston in east Texas produces coiled pine-needle baskets bound with imported raffia, some decorated in synthetic colors (this is also true for the Louisiana Coushatta); cane splintwork has almost ceased to be practiced there. The last three groups have crafts organizations with their own retail stores. Some baskets are produced by other Louisiana tribes. Flexible Houma baskets are of split palmetto; the Chitimacha (Chetimacha), once renowned for fine cane weaving, engage in little basketry now, but I was able to procure the new sewing basket shown in plate 20.

The entire *Pacific Coast* was a fertile region for basketry production. California was the home of numerous tribes skilled in the craft, some of whom are still producing baskets in small quantities but not always in the traditional manner (intertribal marriage has blurred design characteristics and has complicated source assignment) or fine quality. The Pomo, most often named by experts as the greatest historical basketmakers in the world, now have about four craftswomen (some doing feather baskets) and the also-famed Hupa (Hoopa) perhaps ten weavers. A few among the Pit River tribes still make baskets. The occasional old Pomo feathered basket that comes to light is snatched up and priced at a truly impressive figure.

In the Northwest, there was substantial twined or coiled work with roots, barks, and the decorative techniques of false embroidery and imbrication by tribes of Puget Sound and the Cascades Range and Coast-Columbia River regions. A few still weave among the Skokomish,

Chehalis, Quinault, and Lummi of Washington. The technique of wrapped twine, in which two stiff elements, a horizontal and a veritcal, are held together by a flexible weft, is practiced by a few elderly women of the Makahs at Neah Bay on the Olympic Peninsula of Washington. Weaving is mostly done during the excessively rainy winters, and *wabbit* baskets of cedar bark and grasses (pl. 21) are usually made in response to a specific request.

Other than for the Eastern Band of Cherokee and possibly the Passamaquoddy, basketry is today an important income-producing craft only in the *Southwest.* Old Papago (see new miniature of yucca in pl. 11) and Pima coiled baskets with woven-in designs had enough similarities, including the use of willow as material, that they are displayed undifferentiated in a large exhibit case at the Field Museum of Natural History in Chicago. The tribes share a language and probably descend from Hohokam culture ancestors. Bert Robinson's *The Basket Weavers of Arizona* (1954) includes detailed material and photographs covering the work of these tribes and others, as does *Southwest Indian Craft Arts* (1968) by Clara Lee Tanner.

The Hopi produce: coiled plaque trays on Second Mesa (fig. 7); colorful Third Mesa wickerwork plaques or trays of rabbit brush and sumac or wild currant bush, using natural and synthetic dyes; splint-and-wickerwork piki trays for their paper-thin corn bread; and corn sifters (ring baskets) of plaited yucca that are identical to those known to have been woven almost a thousand years ago (pl. 22). The Iroquois had corn washers, but there is no water to waste up on the mesas or in the desert. The sifters screen the grit from kernels that have been parched in hot sand.

The Rio Grande Pueblos of Jémez and Santo Domingo are producing some baskets: from Jémez come split yucca-leaf ring baskets deeper than those of the Hopi, and plate 22 includes an openwork wicker bowl from Santo Domingo that is similar to one shown holding ears of corn in a museum exhibit of a Hopi interior. Shallow versions were once woven to fit rounded-bottom cooking pots, which were stabilized when in use for food storage by resting them in the baskets.

An interesting Western Apache form is the *tus*, a basketry bottle smeared with a thick coating of piñon pitch. The Jicarilla Apaches, whose Spanish-given name means "cup" or "small basket," are again making coiled baskets.

Certainly, there are far fewer living Indian basket forms to study than there were shortly after the turn of the century, when Otis T. Mason and George Wharton James published their classic studies (see Selected Bibliography). Basketry has best survived as a viable craft where it was important economically (Papago and Eastern Band of Cherokee) or figured in the people's everyday lives, as with the Hopi, perhaps the most traditional tribe. The traditional Amerind does not merely live "close to the soil" in the sense that a Midwestern farmer does, but considers himself a part of nature. A Hopi gathers her materials from the earth, lives with and sees her baskets used at table and as valued features of important rituals.

There do exist weavers in tribes commonly presumed no longer to weave. The Navajo, for example, had long purchased their coiled ceremonial bowls, which are exactly prescribed in form and design, from Southern Paiutes and Utes. But in 1973 I encountered a Navajo textile weaver in her thirties who kept balls of yarn in a fine "wedding" basket of her own manufacture. A few months later, I purchased a new specimen that had recently been collected on the Navajo Reservation (pl. 22). Sandra Corrie Newman's book entitled *Indian Basket Weaving* (1974) provided the explanation that the crafts program set up by the Navajo Community College at Many Farms, Arizona, in 1968 had trained sixty basketmakers (with varying levels of expertise, naturally) within three years, where only three had previously possessed the skill.

In this bowl form, the last coil is finished off so that it comes directly opposite the opening in the design that goes from the center to the edge. This represents a path of communication between the lower and upper worlds that must be kept open. Since the basket has to be held with the spirit pathway turned toward the east, finishing off the coil at that point enables the shaman to find it by touch during a nighttime chant, or ceremony. This is by way of offering a bit of the great body of American Indian lore—much of it among the Navajo—about baskets. I'd like to recommend the chapters "Basketry in Indian Legend" and "Basketry in Indian Ceremonial" from George Wharton James's treasure of information about the Southwest, Pacific states, and Alaska, entitled *Indian Basketry* (1909, 1972).

NEW ENGLAND

At the time of the Pilgrims' landing in "New England," the area was populated with approximately twenty-five thousand Algonkin-speaking members of some sixteen tribes organized into loose confederations. Later, pressures from the more aggressive and politically stronger Iroquois nearby, Colonists seeking land, epidemics, two major wars with whites, and involvement by proximity in the French-English struggle over possession were to decimate Algonkian numbers and power.

The Indians welcomed the opportunity to obtain such coveted new goods as woven cloth and metal implements. Barter represented the only means they had, so they offered in exchange wild and cultivated foods, pelts, and baskets. Every Colonial household required an assortment of containers for field and household activities as well as storage.

Cultural exchange took place, and the natives traded techniques with the settlers—for example, teaching the pounding of black ash logs for splint. One Sandwich, New Hampshire, resident remembers that, when she arrived there in 1938, "three or four people were still pounding the brown [black] ash logs and making a few baskets," but that weaving apparently stopped "when the supply of brown ash trees gave out."

The Indians also sold basketry materials, like prepared splint, to non-Indian weavers, among them the Shakers. When white customers demanded sturdy round baskets in standardized sizes so they could do double-duty as measures, the Indians adopted the spider-web bottom and the use of forms or molds. A New England basketry display at the Museum of the American Indian in New York includes fine splint specimens in symmetrical round form, some with a raised bottom and well-carved, high-arched handles that remind us of Shaker work, as well as a feather-type, in which the cover does not come off but is slotted to slide up on the handle.

Intermarriage was common—there are relatively few New Englanders of pure Algonkian blood—and accelerated the back-and-forth shuttling of techniques, so that the matter of who taught or suggested what to whom when resembles a piece of plaited basketry.

Allen H. Eaton, researching his book *Handicrafts of New England* (1949, 1969), found European-born basketmakers (and some of their descendants) producing designs brought from the lands of their birth. These included a considerable number of Finns, some in Vermont, who made birchbark baskets; two Poles, one in Vermont and the other in Massachusetts, who used pine roots; and a Czechoslovakian who had bought a Connecticut farm and found growing there pussy willows like those his family had woven. Splintwork—ash was the commonly used wood—was widespread throughout New England. It is worth noting that similar baskets were traditional in rural areas of the European countries from which most of the immigrants came.

Mr. Eaton was almost thirty years closer to a time when there were basketweaving centers scattered through New England and undertook his research when weavers were still driving truckloads to markets or roadside stands, so his many basket-hunting stories are of no little interest. He talked with a Guilford, Connecticut, man who had learned as a child of eight and, in the ensuing seventy-five years, must have made fifty thousand white oak-splint baskets, probably more than any other New Englander, or American anywhere. Another source [2] quotes a minister who knew Ann Wampy (1760–1836) of the

Pequot Reservation in the vicinity of what is now Ledyard, Connecticut. Each spring she would begin a sales trek, almost hidden under the load of baskets she'd made during the winter. Her baskets were so good that she "would find a customer at almost every house," and would have disposed of the whole load within two or three days.

New England is a treasure trove of old baskets. The three most distinctive types are Algonkian Indian, Shaker, and the Nantucket Lightship Baskets, each discussed elsewhere in this book. Plates 12 and 13 illustrate two Algonkian decorative techniques, the simplest painted decoration, rows of dots, on a handled berry-picking basket, and potato-stamping on a magnificent "bonnet basket" from the Winterthur collection. Plates 42 through 47 show Shaker baskets and plates 48 through 50, Nantucket Lightship Baskets. Plate 23 is of a wood-bottomed basket with movable handle that is a kind of cruder relative to the Nantucket Lightship Baskets. Plates 23 through 40, accompanied by informative captions, cover a wide range of other baskets believed to be of New England origin.

Baskets are still enjoyed in New England, both inherited and new ones; the latter are of splint. One young Connecticut weaver who demonstrates at fairs and crafts shows finds that he sells practically everything he brings and always gets additional orders. Visiting Maine in the fall, I saw splint backpack baskets, favored by hunters, hikers, and the famed Maine guides, hanging outside stores selling them, while some hardware stores featured displays of the local Passamaquoddy utility baskets.

Elsewhere in New England, there are a couple of well-known basket factories offering a variety of shapes and sizes. The recent white ash nailed-rim pie basket in plate 40 is from a New Hampshire firm employing hand labor using some power-driven tools and time-saving methods of manufacture.

SHAKER

The Shaker movement had its beginnings among a sect of English Quakers correctly referred to as The United Society of Believers in

Christ's Second Appearing but who were popularly called the "Shaking Quakers" for their trembling in the unique group dancing that was part of their religious practice. Mother Ann Lee, their head, suffered persecution and imprisonment; then she experienced the vision that sent her to America with eight disciples in 1774. They pioneered wild acreage in New York and not only survived but increased through hard-won converts. Growth continued under able leadership after their leader's death a decade later, and the successful sect's membership had swelled to an estimated six thousand souls in nineteen communities at the movement's peak just before the Civil War.[3]

Austere communal life imposed strict discipline and separation, though equality, of the sexes. The no-nonsense Shakers demanded utility in all things, and their indusrty and reputation for integrity in workmanship and in dealings built an outside market for their goods. They maintained retail shops at their locations; trading deacons went off as traveling salesmen. Prosperity left the Shakers economically well off, and their laborsaving innovations and inventions surely offered more convenience than many in the "world" enjoyed in those days.

Each community was expected to be self-supporting (there was some trading among themselves, of course) and to develop suitable industries to supply its needs and bring in outside income. Most Shaker designs were not really original with them but were simplified and refined versions of extant forms. Their furniture and craft products were the embodiment of suitability and efficiency, displaying purity of line and lack of ornamentation.

In the 1780s Shakers began producing baskets purely for their own use; by 1801, according to Alfred Society account books, they were commonly being offered for sale. Basketry became one of their well-known crafts, a traveler noting in 1842 that: "This sect's baskets are unsurpassed." Eugene Merrick Dodd, then Curator of Hancock Shaker Village, writing on "Functionalism in Shaker Crafts," says: "An account book from the basket shop of the Mount Lebanon community shows that in 1837 at least seventy-six types were produced, ranging from delicate poplar sewing baskets three inches in diameter to split black ash baskets six feet long for carrying and storing barks, roots, and herbs." [4] The Shakers' reliance on diversified agriculture and home industries, such as the seed and pharmaceutical businesses, required quantities of baskets made for specific applications.

Although versatility was encouraged—one Brother's diary indicated that he had in one day tailored a coat, farmed, and engaged in craftwork—those who joined as adults brought their talents and skills with them, often continuing to do the same jobs they had before. It was logical, for example, for the Pleasant Hill, Kentucky, Shakers to make willow baskets, for they and the Ohio Believers were culturally rooted in Virginia, North Carolina, and Pennsylvania, states where the material was commonly used, as it was elsewhere in Kentucky. The Pleasant Hill collection includes a large-openwork willow basket, resembling a later Southern Highlands example in figure 16, and a good-sized oval covered one with swing handles similar to that in plate 7.

Strict separation of the sexes included the pursuit of industries, so that one couldn't have found Shaker Brethren and Sisters working side by side in the basket shop. At Pleasant Hill, it was a Sisters' craft, but men probably made the bigger and heavier baskets in at least some communities.

The Eastern communities (New York and New England) had much contact with neighboring Indians, who sometimes helped them learn or improve upon their basketry techniques. Although there do not seem to have been Indian converts, the Shakers did evangelize among them and trade with them. The Shaker Museum (Old Chatham, New York) accession card for an oval basket with flexible handles (similar to that at right front in pl. 7) comments on its European design influence and notes that the handles are wrapped in ash bought from the Indians. Also at The Shaker Museum, which has a superb collection of Shaker baskets, almost all of them on display, is a group of Mahican (Algonkian) potato-stamped baskets. When such have come out of Shaker communities or connections, they have often been mistakenly identified as Shaker, when, in fact, there is no indication that Shakers incorporated block-stamped (and almost never colored) weavers into their baskets. The Sabbathday Lake Community does have baskets that have been painted all over the outside only.

The Shakers did not label or sign their baskets, and there were no instruction manuals. Objects sometimes carried the initials "S. C." indicating use in a Shaker Community, and letters combined with numbers were used to show placement—for example, "M7" for Ministry building, Room 7. The Shakers employed many woods, including hickory, black ash, some oak, and finely cut poplar. They almost invariably wove over molds, which helps explain the symmetrical shapes, but tended to use thicker splints than the local Indians. Well-made New England specimens can be found that closely resemble baskets in Shaker collections, and, without proof of provenance, positive identification is all but impossible. One former Brother lived out his last years as a professional basketmaker on the outside. Perhaps he came to the Shakers with the skill, perhaps not, but the nagging question whether his later baskets should be considered Shaker might well arise.

There is no such thing as a Shaker *weave,* but materials were usually carefully prepared and construction was sound. In using one's eye to judge whether a basket *could* be Shaker, and this is what professionals do, the tendency is to measure it against known examples of their finest work. Plate 42 features a group of the kind of elegant splint baskets that we're inclined to think of as the "real" Shaker baskets. They display simplicity of line and well-carved, high, rigid handles, some have the often-found raised bottom and wrapped (commonly double-wrapped or cross-bound, but far from always so) rim that we have come to associate with Shaker work.

But it is unrealistic to expect every Shaker basket to be fine. The collection at Hancock Shaker Village, which has a firm policy about not using any reproductions in historical or cultural exhibits, includes a great variety of construction, nailed rims among them. Their Basket Shop is photographed in figure 12, and lots of baskets have been

FIGURE 12. Basket Shop at Hancock Shaker Village. The exhibit includes a collection of wooden molds on the shelves at rear, riving and shaving tools for slitting and smoothing the splints, and a form on which a handle or hoop is being shaped. Almost all Shaker baskets were woven over molds, which helps to explain the usual symmetry of their splintwork. Photograph courtesy Hancock Shaker Village, Hancock, Massachusetts.

placed in appropriate settings such as the Herb-Drying Room (fig. 13).

Familiar Shaker forms include handled rectangular baskets (pls. 43 and 46) and the large hamper in plate 44, which came from the Loom Room at North Church Family, Mount Lebanon, New York. Hexagonal openwork cheese curd baskets were made by and are connected with the Shakers, who sold them, but few realize that the weave was used for kitchen storage baskets (see the handled egg basket of pl. 45). The pharmaceutical display at The Shaker Museum at Old Chatham contains a divided tray for six bottles; although the weavers vary in width, an Indian technique, the thicker splints point to non-Indian manufacture. The fancy picnic hamper with divided, hinged lid (pl. 47) was doubtless made for sale to the "carriage trade"; it may well owe its design inspiration to China Trade baskets like the one in figure 14.

Shaker enrollment and prosperity began to decline sharply beginning in the 1870s. As communities had to be closed, goods were distributed to contacts, sold through auction, or sent to surviving

FIGURE 13. Herb-Drying Room at Hancock Shaker Village. A quantity and diversity of genuine Shaker baskets is displayed here and elsewhere throughout the village. The museum has a very firm policy about not using any reproductions in historical or cultural exhibits. Photograph courtesy Hancock Shaker Village, Hancock, Massachusetts.

communities, which found themselves with a surfeit of things, including the durable baskets.

The Shaker Museum at Sabbathday Lake, a living residential community located near Poland Spring, Maine, has a comprehensive collection of perhaps three hundred Shaker and some local Indian-made baskets, the bulk of them in storage at this writing. Part of the now-demolished Great Mill was sometimes used for basketmaking. Most of the collection consists of baskets that never left the community; it is believed that the Indian examples were acquired when they arrived holding purchased goods.

Marian Klamkin's *Hands to Work: Shaker Folk Art and Industries* (1972) illustrates a number of sewing baskets made of a handloom-woven, strawlike poplar fabric manufactured by the Sisters, which was also used for other items sold in quantity in their shops into the twentieth century. However, commercial basketweaving had ceased by 1880.

NANTUCKET LIGHTSHIP BASKETS

Other than for fine old Indian baskets, these are our most expensive collectors' pieces, specimens in good condition costing several hundred dollars. A nest of eight, made and labeled by A. D. Williams of Nantucket in 1922, was offered at forty-five hundred dollars in the June 1974 issue of The Magazine *Antiques*.

The South Shoal Lightship or Light-Vessel was established in the mid-1850s off tiny Nantucket Island, Massachusetts, which had been a world-leading whaling port during the early 1840s. (Offshore whaling had been succeeded by a whale fishery relying on large ships capable of voyages lasting years, but whaling was dead by 1870 as the result of several occurrences, most notably the discovery of petroleum.)

Tours of duty aboard the lightship, a very small craft anchored where a lighthouse is needed but cannot be built because of the difficult location, could take eight months, during which the sailors had few chores aside from tending the lights. Some of the seamen on this particular ship took to weaving sturdy baskets of imported rattan

—caning, made from the tough stems of a tropical climbing palm—over hickory or oak ribs. The thin ribs were inserted firmly into a deep slot near the edge of a pliable turned-wood base or bottom board to achieve a strong joint.

Forms were round or oval, woven on molds, and often made in nesting sets. They had movable handles attached to a pair of ears (pls. 48–50). A different form was a shallow round basket with a pair of short, rigid handles at the rim. The old-timers usually did not put any finish on the baskets, which accounts for their deeply brown tones. When a finish was used, it was likely to be a light varnishing that retarded the browning/aging process and that also gave a gloss.

The sale of the baskets provided supplemental income for the men. Some became both skilled and prolific, as was Captain Charles B. Ray, who is known to have completed two hundred baskets by 1866. Although durable, a good many of the handsome baskets were kept as display pieces and never saw other service.

A cruder relative but reminiscent of the Nantucket Lightship Baskets is the wood-bottomed, movable-handled, nailed-rim example in plate 23; a knowledgeable antiques dealer says such baskets are called "New Hampshire baskets" and are considered forerunners of the Nantucket Lightship work. The matter of antecedents seems to be arguable; some suggest Indian influence, undeniably pervasive throughout the Northeast, but others note the strong Quaker environment. Allen H. Eaton, in *Handicrafts of New England* (1949, 1969), quotes an authority pointing out that similar baskets had been made for generations in a Quaker colony on the "continent." Katherine and Edgar Seeler, in *Nantucket Lightship Baskets* (1972), offer an excerpt from an author contemporary to the Lightship period proving earlier manufacture of what were then called *rattan baskets*. A strong tradition of handcrafts, including woodworking and coopering existed among the sailors and whalemen (they called recreational handwork *scrimshawing*), who found themselves isolated during protracted periods of idle time.

It is certain that many who never served on the Nantucket Lightship wove similar baskets on land during the Lightship period;

after weaving aboard had ceased, about 1895, it continued on Nantucket Island. Experts differ concerning the significance of grooved circles in the wooden base as a clue to identification of the makers. An authority who is shortly bringing out a book believes that the grooving of numbers of circles into the base was merely an idiosyncrasy of individual basketmakers, many of whom bought bottoms turned by others and had different patterns from time to time. Some weavers affixed labels, many of which have been lost, to their pieces; stencils were also employed. Names burned into the bases of old baskets may be those of either owners or weavers.

In the 1940s a Filipino immigrant began weaving Nantucket Lightship Baskets, which he made with a cover so that they might be used as women's purse baskets. The wife of a carver thought to add an ivory decoration, such as a whale or sea gull, to the lid's wooden center. (The most expensive ivory is whale tooth, which has tan streaks and is now prohibited elsewhere, but white elephant ivory is also used, as is whalebone.)

There are perhaps half a dozen craftsmen working full-time at making covered and some "open baskets," as they call the traditional forms. One weaver made the careful distinction that these are not reproductions because the making of the Nantucket Lightship Baskets had never ceased and has been a continuing craft. It is usual for modern weavers to burn or incise their names into the turned bases, which may be purchased from others, and baskets are finished with several coats of varnish and/or sealer. Informal demonstrations are held by some who sell from their homes. Costing almost as much as older Nantucket Lightship Baskets, the new handbags have proven a popular status symbol and are being imitated.

The Peter Foulger Museum of the Nantucket Historical Association displays two cases of the Lightship Baskets.

SOUTHEASTERN PENNSYLVANIA

German-speaking Colonists wanting religious freedom and the chance for a better living began emigrating to Pennsylvania, one of the original thirteen states, in the late seventeenth century. Although they spread through all the state, the heaviest concentration occurred in the southeastern portion. They were farmers and craftsmen, some of whom made coiled rye-straw baskets. These were often referred to as *beehive* baskets, because European apiarists had long utilized such hives or skeps to protect their bees from freezing in winter.

The Pennsylvania Germans (incorrectly called "Dutch") put these baskets to a wide range of uses, the principal two being storage and as dough-raising/bread baskets. Large covered hampers held clothing and food, commonly cheesecloth bags of sun-dried fruits; those for cut-up dried apples were swelling vase-shapes called *schnitz* baskets. After bread was kneaded and formed into loaves, they were placed in uncovered shallow bowl-baskets to rise overnight. These were sometimes oval or great, round ones. Smaller examples might have one or two handles for hanging, formed by pulling out and binding the last coil away from the body (pl. 51). Bindings were narrow hickory or white oak splints. Coiled-straw baskets—wheat and oat straw were others—were made by Germans elsewhere, in Virginia and Ohio, for example.

Demonstrations are given at the Ephrata Cloisters, Ephrata, Pennsylvania, and some coiled rye-straw baskets are being produced today. The very few basketmakers who sell their products have more than enough orders; one stated that it took him about four hours to produce a small basket and up to twenty hours for a large one.

Other basketry materials were splint and willow rods. White oak-splint baskets were commonly of the rib-type, often the "splitting" or "buttocks" form, with splint handle (the example in pl. 53 has a double-splint handle). Uses around the farm and house were legion, and various sizes offered convenience for chores and gathering produce, as well as acting as measures. Osiers were woven into sturdy laundry baskets and round, handled Lancaster County market baskets, no longer being made locally of local materials. Baskets that are sold at the Lancaster and Reading markets and elsewhere in Lancaster and Berks Counties are imports or of imported materials.

Cornelius Weygandt, author of *The Dutch Country* (1939), notes

FIGURE 14. Chinese rice-straw basket sometimes mistaken for Pennsylvania German: nineteenth century. A product of the China Trade, with polychrome spot-painted floral decorations and separate cover fitting tightly into the rim, such baskets were so often found among Pennsylvania "Dutch" that they came to be associated with them and have even been assumed to be of local manufacture. Their light weight is deceptive, for the skillful construction proves unexpectedly strong. H. 4¼"; L. 9⅜"; D. 5¼". Photograph courtesy The Henry Francis du Pont Winterthur Museum, Winterthur, Delaware.

that these home-centered immigrants lavished great care in the making of special little Christmas and Easter egg baskets for children. Unusual handles might be applied, splints dyed, or baskets woven of two materials, all to be as eye-catchingly different as possible from the everyday baskets all about them. Some were hung upon the Chrisitmas tree loaded with sweets or put under it. The children might leave coiled rye-straw baskets in the chimney corners to be filled with gifts and goodies.

Figure 14 shows a China Trade covered basket of rice straw with spot-painted floral decoration, a type once so common in the Pennsylvania German area that it has sometimes mistakenly been assumed to be local in origin. Earl F. Robacker in *Touch of the Dutchland* (1965), points out that their light look and weight belie the strength given by skillful construction.

An excellent collection of basketwares, probably most of them originating in southeastern Pennsylvania, is exhibited at the Pennsylvania Farm Museum of Landis Valley, Lancaster (see pl. 52 of a group made of coiled straw). Included are unusual specimens, such as the large, flat-backed pair of what are presumed to be American later eighteenth century or early nineteenth century horse or mule pack baskets (pl. 54) because of their resemblance to those in European engravings. Two football-shaped wicker baskets (pl. 55), described by the Landis brothers' records as nut-gathering baskets, are known in Canada as woolgathering baskets, into which the thrifty shepherd-farmer would tuck the bits of wool left by his charges on thorny bushes and pasture fence lines.

COASTAL SOUTH

The basketweaving demonstrations informally held at the Colonial Williamsburg restoration of Virginia are widely known. A working Basketmaker's Shop employs two weavers, one taught by Mr. and Mrs. William Cody Cook, who were resident there during the late 1960s and into 1971. Figure 15 is a still from an excellent film produced at Williamsburg, *Basketmaking in Colonial Virginia*, featuring the Cooks making a white oak-splint, eighteenth-century-type service basket.

The Williamsburg basketweavers are supplied with white oak logs and prepare splint by hand, using a knife to start the splints. Hoops (rims) are cross-bound; they call it "double-lashing." Round baskets are woven with flat bottoms and then punched in with the fist to form a raised center "so it sets flat," even when fully loaded. Hundreds of their baskets in several forms are sold each year in the Prentis and the Tarpley's Stores in the Historic Area.

Plate 56 shows a split-oak covered sewing basket by Mr. Roy Black (the first he made with three small handles) and a square peck by the Cooks. Plate 57 is of a basket with forked handle ends, presumed to have been woven by the Cooks during their stay at Williamsburg.

A number of baskets, including round poultry cages I had never seen, have been placed in appropriate settings or are in use in exhibits. Baskets had to be acquired, so it should not be assumed that they have been authenticated. In fact, curatorial staff research failed to locate any non-Indian baskets of Colonial date and Virginia origin, nor could information be retrieved about whether any were even made in the town. Quite a few references in estate inventories and advertisements did describe baskets as being of split oak.

Westville, near Lumpkin, Georgia, is a village of relocated and restored buildings depicting the handicrafts and culture of Georgia around 1850. There are basketmakers in the area, and weaving of white oak splint is demonstrated, including that of cotton basket forms.

The ubiquitous cotton basket was found on all southern plantations and farms in the nineteenth century. Placed in the fields at the ends of the rows, the pickers dumped their sacks into it, and the loaded basket was then carried to the wagon. The cotton basket was of split white oak or ash, had a square or round bottom, depending on local custom, a round mouth, and usually had slots just under the rim into which the fingers could be slipped. In eastern Texas, these baskets were made almost exclusively by blacks for sale to farmers, but one elderly "German" farmer near Austin had been taught to weave them by his father, who had learned from blacks.

A researcher has offered other information about basketry in Texas: A check of the 1850, 1860, and 1870 census returns found no one who described himself as a basketmaker or basketweaver. Galveston newspapers of the 1850s and 1860s carried ads for vast quantities of "willoware" being imported into the state by wholesalers. I understand that there are stories of Mexican-American basketweaving in the communities along the Rio Grande sixty or seventy years ago, but these have not been documented with examples of their work.

A 1975 trip into Louisiana and Mississippi located several men, almost all of them black, who were producing oak-splint utility baskets for local farmers' egg- and vegetable-gathering chores and for the hand-picking of cotton. One craftsman, who had been taught by his

FIGURE 15. Mr. and Mrs. William Cody Cook, former resident basketweavers at Colonial Williamsburg (1965–1971). Mr. Cook prepares white oak splints using a knife to start the split and assist in the pulling operation that separates the natural wood layers. Next, Mrs. Cook trims, scrapes, and smooths the splints. This is a still from the film *Basketmaking in Colonial Virginia*. Photograph courtesy the Colonial Williamsburg Collection, Williamsburg, Virginia.

father and has been in business thirty-odd years, hangs outside his shop on the Main Street of a small town the sign: "_____'s Weaving Shop & Basketmaking of All Sizes."

I found Acadian (Cajun) palmetto baskets of stitched-together bands plaited from strips of the cutout center (that is, new growth just before it opens) of a young plant. A woman informant had learned the three-day curing and weaving of the eighteen- to twenty-four-inch splints as a child and remembered watching the ladies make themselves broad-brimmed hats. The Houma tribe of Louisiana also plait palmetto baskets and mats. Other tribes in that state coil pine needles or a native grass and weave cane or white oak; their work and that of the Eastern Band of Choctaws in Mississippi and the Alabama and Coushatta Tribes of east Texas are taken up in the "Southeast" portion of this volume's "American Indian" section.

Coiled baskets of sweet grass have been made by Afro-Americans of the Sea Islands region since their arrival on this continent two hundred years ago. This craft, which survives among the Gullah blacks of the Mount Pleasant area near Charleston, South Carolina, is discussed next.

GULLAH AFRO-AMERICAN

A few-mile stretch along U. S. Highway 17 north of Mount Pleasant near Charleston attests to the vigor of a basketmaking tradition that bears strong evidence of African influence. On agreeable days during the tourist season, black women demonstrate their craft and sell their work from dozens of roadside stands, actually wooden racks set out in front of their homes or at other locations, which are manned by relatives. Some of the larger stands are open the year around, although few are attended on Sunday because most of these religious people set that day aside for churchgoing and visiting.

Gullah Afro-Americans maintain a personal culture with unique aspects and customs and even its own dialect. The origin of the name *Gullah* for blacks of the Sea Islands and coastal regions of South

Carolina, Georgia, and northeastern Florida is much disputed by scholars, but one of the more generally accepted theories is that it refers back to *Ngola*, hereditary title of the chiefs of a West Coast African kingdom, from which word probably derived the name of Angola, a former Portuguese colony once active in the slave trade.

Documented by example as early as 1730, Afro-American baskets were common on southern plantations by 1850. A large, round coiled basket is in the foreground of a Civil War photograph showing blacks, some in cast-off army uniforms, planting sweet potatoes on a plantation abandoned by its owners. The Gullah baskets stylistically resemble American Museum of Natural History (New York) examples from Angola, about 1900, and recent coiled baskets from the Senegal-Gambia area, so much so that a South Carolina specimen in the above museum's Man in Africa Hall exhibit could be mislabeled as a Senegalese counterpart. It is interesting to consider that the Senegal-Gambia section of Africa provided a third of South Carolina's slave population between 1752 and 1808, with the remaining two-thirds from the Congo-Angola area.[5] A new Ovambo basket, from a tribe living in a territory covering part of both Angola and Southwest Africa, resembles Gullah work, even to the decorative incorporation of dark brown fibers. Slave-made round *fanna* (fanner) baskets for the winnowing of rice, specimens of which may be seen at Charles Towne Landing and the Old Slave Mart Museum, both in Charleston, link traditional African basketry to its craft survival as contemporary American Gullah work. A close-up of a basket in the Smithsonian Institution (pl. 58) shows the coiling.

Core material consists of bundles of a long, slender, sweet-smelling grass that grows near the coast along the edges of marshes and tidal streams—some weavers call it "sea straw"—with brown longleaf pine needles woven in for decorative effect. The sweet grass, which rather smells like hay, is green when harvested and dries pale golden. Some like to work in the thicker, dark gold "rushel," a tough rush that was added for strength to the fanna baskets. The only tool, other than scissors or a knife for cutting, is a spoon handle from which the bowl has been broken and the rough end filed to a wedge or chisel shape.

It is utilized as an awl, to punch openings in the coil for the sewing (binding) fiber, always strips of split palmetto fronds.

Both boys and girls learn the technique from their mothers and grandmothers and help by gathering the materials. Later, only women pursue the craft, except for an occasional man unfit for other work. In Africa, too, basketry is considered women's work. The elderly maker of a large covered piece stated that it was the only work she could now do and that it had taken four days; the price was eighteen dollars. Gullah baskets are seldom available through shops or antiques dealers. The craft is admittedly endangered because, as land development removes more and more coastal acreage from its wild state, the artisans are losing their nearby supply of grass.

Although dozens of forms are offered, the best are those most clearly retaining African design influence, such as those in plate 59, all collected by the author in 1974. Others have been adapted to sell: trays for glasses, mats, various purse baskets, hanging or wall baskets, fruit and flower baskets, some with openwork bands or borders. The knob frequently topping covers is a distinctive feature. Called a "nipple," it is sometimes hollow so that a finger may be inserted to facilitate removing the lid.

SOUTHERN APPALACHIAN HIGHLANDS

An invaluable assist to identifying regional origins of basket forms is gained by firsthand examination of new work. Where there has been continuity of tradition, as there has been in the Southern Appalachian Highlands, commonly designated Appalachia, one may find, for example, a new handled tray similar to an older one in plate 60. Excellent basketweaving continues in the region, but the small number of mostly elderly weavers—other than among the Cherokee—may seem surprising in view of the fact that so much basketmaking was being done when Allen H. Eaton's *Handicrafts of the Southern Highlands* was first published in 1937.

He knew quite a few of the best craftworkers of the day, including Aunt Cord Ritchie of Hindman, Kentucky, who is shown with four of her baskets in a Doris Ulmann photograph (fig. 16). She taught herself by taking apart a basket from "over the mountains," experimenting, and developing her own designs and plant dyes. A thriving basketry craft existed in Kentucky in the 1930s, but very little remains. Hindman, in Knott County, has a school that was once the center for basketmaking activity, but none survives there. Southwestern Kentuckians must have needed and missed being able to get baskets back in 1960, when an Arkansas weaver drove to Fulton to sell a truckload of a week's work of plaited white oak baskets.

The Kentucky Guild of Artists & Craftsmen counted one active basketmaker among its members in 1974. (There are a few basketweavers not affiliated with the Guild.) The Guild holds an annual fair at Berea, Kentucky, its headquarters, and has a retail gallery outlet in Lexington. The Berea College Appalachian Museum, devoted to the traditional life-style of the area, displays a group of old baskets. Some new ones are available through the Log House Sales Room on the campus.

The Southern Highlands consists of the Appalachian Mountains region of western Maryland and Virginia, most of West Virginia, eastern Kentucky and Tennessee, western North Carolina, northwestern South Carolina, northern Georgia, and northeastern Alabama. Arriving from southern Pennsylvania and eastern Virginia and North Carolina, the great majority of new settlers were of Anglo-Saxon ancestry. The Cherokee of North Carolina are descendants of those who successfully eluded and fought forcible removal to Oklahoma in the late 1830s and finally won the legal right to remain.

The Appalachian tradition is one of independence, for the pioneers endured a hard, lonely frontier existence, isolated in misleadingly beautiful coves and valleys, to wring a generally lean living from poor soil. Of necessity, they used their hands to shape native materials into log cabins, furniture, clothing, tools, and household goods. A craft such as basketry gave a mountaineer something to barter for a few essential supplies from the nearest store.

Rib-type baskets of varying forms, the prevalent construction even today and one adopted by the Cherokee, comprise plate 61. A variant of the Carolina basket (pl. 63), identified by Allen H. Eaton as an early twentieth-century design, is produced by the Cherokee with a stabilizing round base and is called a knitting basket. The oriole of plate 64, presumably named for its resemblance to that bird's hanging sacklike nest, was referred to by Eaton as a Kentucky egg basket, one of the oldest designs, with the long, flat sides intended to rest against the horse or mule's shoulder. But what is being called a Kentucky egg basket today is shown by an example from Golden ("Bunt") Howard (pl. 60).

White oak is the wood now used. There was some hickory splint in the past, and a little round-rod willow or honeysuckle vine weaving is still being done (in Kentucky); otherwise, the Cherokee excepted, weaving is of natural white oak splint. Only during the crafts revival at the beginning of this century did non-Indian weavers extensively incorporate colored bands dyed with vegetal stains, although a little walnut dyeing is currently being done in the area and in the Ozarks.

Although the local people buy and use baskets, these do not represent the bulk of sales. The Southern Highland Handicraft Guild was established in 1930 and dedicated to preserving, improving, and marketing mountain crafts, the latter a serious stumbling block for so many remote artisans. Headquartered in Asheville, North Carolina, the guild operates four retail outlet shops for members' work and sponsors two annual Craftsman's Fairs, at Asheville in July and at Gatlinburg, Tennessee, in October.

FIGURE 16. Aunt Cord Ritchie of Hindman, Kentucky: believed to be c. 1931. A teacher of many neighbors but self-taught, these examples prove her versatility with forms and materials. She originated designs and prepared dyes from willow and hemlock barks. Although she used white oak and hickory splints and other fibers, willow was her favorite. She once said that she could not live where willows did not grow. Photograph courtesy the Doris Ulmann Foundation and Berea College, Berea, Kentucky.

Among its members is the Qualla Arts and Crafts Mutual, Incorporated, of the Eastern Band of Cherokee Indians. The official display and marketing center at Cherokee, North Carolina, offers a selection of hundreds of fine baskets at retail. Plate 18 shows contemporary examples of white oak splint, wild honeysuckle vine, and plaited river cane, mostly dyed with root stains. Basketry is recognized as the leading Cherokee craft (about one hundred and fifty weave), and exhibitions, including individual shows for leading practitioners, are held.

Demonstrations are presented at the Oconaluftee Indian Village in Cherokee during its season. The Museum of the Cherokee Indian, also at Cherokee, has a collection of baskets.

MIDWEST

The agricultural Midwest offers good basket hunting for specimens of the simple-but-honest kind, like the hickory splint from Illinois included in plate 65. I have found that Ohio sources yield a good quantity and quality of local baskets, two examples of which are included in that plate; another is shown in plate 67.

Truly a basket for the ages is a hickory apple basket from Michigan, reinforced with a rivet through the base (pl. 68). A produce basket with the highest raised bottom I have ever seen, five inches (pl. 69), is at the Chicago Historical Society. Not pretty, strictly functional, is the twenty-eight-inch long peeled-willow meat delivery basket that worked for a Chicago wholesaler during the earliest part of the twentieth century (pl. 71).

The Midwest was quite a melting pot. Ohio, for example, held several Shaker communities; colonies of German-speaking Dunkards, Mennonites, and Amish who moved to the western part of the state, mostly from Pennsylvania but some from Virginia, as churches of perhaps eighteen or twenty families each; and Algonkian Indians who had been pushed from their lands farther east. One finds much of their early twentieth-century splintwork in Ohio, but there is no indication of current weaving. Ohio Algonkian baskets are included in plate 16 with others of tribes from the western Great Lakes region.

A large, creel-shaped covered basket with hand-forged hinges (pl. 72) was acquired from a Nebraska dealer; it may have sailed here with a Scandinavian immigrant. Western Ohio and east-central Indiana once yielded the coiled rye-straw baskets characteristically found in German-speaking communities. One collector acquired several in Ohio and has a childhood recollection of hearing about a full-time professional who lived by the creek in Brandt, Ohio, and specialized in them in the late 1800s.

Quite a number of old splint farm baskets turn up in Illinois, so many from certain areas that one suspects that they were the homes of basketweaving families. Plate 70 shows a tall, covered hamper collected in that state. Some rib-type wickerwork baskets of willow rods also turn up. Despite evidence of substantial earlier basketmaking activity, an Illinois museum curator has been unable to locate a present-day artisan to demonstrate the skill at folk-life festivals. In fact, it would appear that the only traditional basketry being done now in the Great Lakes states of the Midwest is that by craftworkers of the Winnebago, Menomini, Ottawa, and Chippewa tribes living in Wisconsin and Michigan.

AMANA COLONIES OF IOWA

The Amana Colonies, a group of seven villages twenty miles west of Iowa City and southwest of Cedar Rapids, were founded by settlers of German, Swiss, and Alsatian ancestry who fled religious persecution to settle in New York State in 1842. In Europe, the sect called itself The Community of True Inspirationists, the Ebenezer Society when in New York, and, after moving to Iowa in 1855, the Amana Society from the biblical name meaning "remain faithful." Within the twenty-six thousand fertile prairie acres purchased, the villages totaling eight hundred people were spaced for convenience in tending the farm lands, but within a six-mile radius of Amana.

The Amanas did almost no trading with the outside. Each village was virtually self-sufficient, containing a communal kitchen and dining hall, as well as a bakery, slaughterhouse, blacksmith shop, general store, and basketweaver's shop. Each family lived together in its own quarters but needed no kitchen because all food preparation was communal. One of my favorite photographs is of a neat row of sun-bonneted women husking corn together. Set before them are baskets of the "bushel" and deep types holding the ears.

Jobs were assigned at age fourteen, when children completed schooling. Able-bodied or skilled young men were needed for all the heavier agricultural or crafts duties, so it was common for older or handicapped men (always men) to be assigned more sedentary tasks like basketmaking. Basket requisitions were filled as needed and frugal repairs made if at all possible. Weaving was interrupted when extra farmhands were needed and at harvest.

Quantities of wickerwork willow baskets were produced, the unpeeled variety for the field and the peeled for indoors, with combinations of the two for decorative effect. Types made included apple-picking (fig. 10—smaller versions could be worn at the waist, held by a belt pulled through a pair of handles close together at the rim), field (either the quite common "bushel" or large-capacity deep type, some with three handles), laundry, knitting (round, some with fancier wrapped handle), market or shopping, and the *liebesbrot* church communion-bread basket that was big enough to accommodate the substantial pieces communicants received then. There were two distinguishing features: a base border that saved wear and tear on the bottom and could be easily replaced when it wore out, and a technique that alternated peeled and unpeeled osiers and passed all osiers of each kind over and under the same ribs to result in vertical lines of dark and light. The twisted handles used in pairs at the rim of some baskets are of split willow, some twisted over a withe. The fiber is not boiled to soften it, and there's supposed to be a "trick" to making them.

Not surprisingly, the wickerwork resembles that of the Pennsylvania Germans. It is believed that the rye-straw and rib-type baskets occasionally found in the colonies were brought there. The only known Amana-made splintwork are the Shoup baskets, woven well over a century ago for their maker's own purposes. The hard-to-find Shoup baskets, made from "plants cut along the [Iowa] river" (even now, the wood is slightly greenish—it may be poplar), are highly prized by collectors within the colonies. One is included in plate 73 with others collected in 1973. Although uncounted thousands of the sturdy Amana baskets were produced, they rarely surface today and are not easily acquired.

Such industries as the woolen mills and furniture factory continue, but crafts like basketmaking were in a decline before the "Great Change" of 1932, when a vote of the people ended the communal system in favor of the adoption of free enterprise. The only baskets woven since have been a very few made privately, and the only Amana resident able to do so—although never a basketmaker by trade —has ceased making them. A small, interested group has started a patch of basket willows and hopes to revive the craft in West Amana. The Museum of Amana History in the Village of Amana displays an excellent collection of various types of old Amana baskets.

OZARKS

No unique basket forms indigenous to the Ozark Mountains region of northern Arkansas and southern Missouri are known. Basketmaking was not practiced by the Osage or Missouri Indians who made up the majority of the area's early population (source: Arkansas State University Museum, Jonesboro). After the Indian removal by the federal government, the area began to be resettled during the mid-nineteenth century. A good many new Ozarkers came from the Southern Appalachians (particularly Tennessee) and brought those traditions with them. Basketmaking was one, although the craft does not seem to have been especially active until recent years.

In 1961, as part of the rural development program designed to expand jobs in home industry, a delegation of forty community leaders and five Cooperative Extension Service staff members went to Gatlinburg, Tennessee, to study the operation of the Southern Highland Handicraft Guild. Upon their return, the Ozark Foothills Handicraft Guild was organized. With its home office at Heber Springs and retail shops there and at Clinton and Hardy, the Arkansas guild, which sponsors annual craft shows at Mountain View in April and Heber Springs in October, numbered ten basketweavers among its members in 1973.

Workshops are conducted in cooperation with the local Vo-Tech School, and, since basketry was a craft revival, the few teachers have strongly influenced forms. The plaited white oak-splint baskets (some hickory and ash were formerly used) exhibit such features as twilled plaiting of square-lined bottoms; a base border on some round ones, a legacy from the teacher from whom most of the recent Arkansas weavers learned and a detail rarely found elsewhere today; and well-carved handles. Some weavers are using imported flat reed, which can easily be mistaken for white oak splint, because it is inexpensive and saves a lot of work. The fiber is woven over white oak ribs, with the rough side in and the smooth, slightly shiny side out. Several years ago, craftsmen used buckbush (coral berry, a woody vine) and also worked with pine needles and sedge grass (broom sedge).

Although no baskets of rib-type construction are being produced in Arkansas, a Missouri couple who are third-generation basketmakers produce a variety of round and oval rib-baskets rather resembling the picnic hamper at the left in plate 62. Plate 74 shows new baskets collected in the Arkansas Ozarks. Two are from the Gibson family, whose tradition says that a blind basketweaver taught an ancestor, and who live in the northwestern part of the state. The Ozark Native Craft Association, Inc., established to assist mountain artisans who lacked a year-round market, has its headquarters and sales outlet in Brentwood, also in northwestern Arkansas.

A 1962 study by a graduate student in the Department of Sociology and Anthropology at the University of Missouri in Columbia found that Ozarks basketmaking techniques ranged from the completely archaic—the clue is in hand-tearing of splints—to those of craftsmen who relied more on power tools, even to having straight-grained logs cut into prepared boards at a sawmill.[6] A common Ozarks tool is a homemade, double-handled split-cutting knife. The thickness of the splint can be controlled with adjustable screws, and a guide assures uniformity. The split-cutting knife is pulled along the edge of a board, which is held in a vise, in one continuous stroke. It can cut wider splints than can comfortably be torn by hand, so that fewer weavers are needed to fill a basket.

Craft demonstrations, basketmaking among them, are held during the season at the State Parks Division–run Ozark Folk Center at Mountain View, and pleasant accommodations in duplex lodges are available to visitors. A commercial enterprise called Silver Dollar City, located near Branson in southwestern Missouri, also conducts split-oak basketry demonstrations.

PACIFIC COAST

The story of Pacific Coast basketry seems to be that of its Indian tribes, although relatively little basketmaking persists in California and the Northwest today. One interesting basket being woven by a few elderly women of the Makah, a Nootka tribe centered at Neah Bay on the Olympic Peninsula, is the *wabbit* basket in plate 21. The only basket the Makahs buy and use themselves, it carries family dishes to a potlatch. At the conclusion of the party, the dirty dishes and all the *wabbit*—the word translates "leftover"—the participant wants are loaded into the basket and taken home. The shape, round or square, is a matter of preference. A smaller, "floppy-handled" version intended for lighter loads is popular because it is easier to slip under the chairs or benches in the community hall where the potlatches are held.

The early Spanish Franciscan Missions in California produced a small quantity of wine for sacramental use and employed Indian laborers who probably used baskets of their own manufacture to harvest grapes. An early 1870s photograph of the champagne-bottling operation being conducted under the open sky at the Buena Vista (originally Haraszthy) Vineyard includes handled wicker divided carriers for the bottles and a covered hamper that may have held the group's lunch. The baskets have a European look and may have been made by foreign-born workers who might also have produced gathering baskets. Inquiries to a number of likely sources have failed to locate any old grape baskets or information about their manufacture or use in the California wine industry.

In general, the West Coast, being a more recently settled portion of the United States, probably had factory-made stave baskets by the time any appreciable number of containers were needed in its developing agriculture.

NOTES

1. Rodney L. Leftwich, *Arts and Crafts of the Cherokee* (Cullowhee, N.C.: Land-of-the-Sky Press, 1970).
2. Eva L. Butler, "Some Early Indian Basket Makers of Southern New England," p. 40 in an Addendum to Frank G. Speck's *Eastern Algonkian Block-Stamp Decoration: A New World Original or an Acculturated Art*, Research Series No. 1. See note 4, page 47.
3. Charles W. Upton, "The Shaker Utopia," *Antiques* (October 1970). Reprinted by permission of The Magazine *Antiques*.
4. Eugene Merrick Dodd, "Functionalism in Shaker Crafts," *Antiques* (October 1970). Reprinted by permission of The Magazine *Antiques*.
5. Elsa Honig Fine, *The Afro-American Artist* (New York: Holt, Rinehart and Winston, Inc., 1973), p. 14.
6. John Robert Vincent, "A Study of Two Ozark Woodworking Industries" (Graduate thesis presented to the faculty of the Department of Sociology and Anthropology, University of Missouri, Columbia, June 1962).

4.

Collecting

RESEARCH

Although this is the first collector's book devoted entirely to hand-woven American "working" baskets, several writers on ethnic, communal, or regional handicrafts have included chapters or sections on basketry. These works are listed in the Selected Bibliography, as are volumes dealing with Indian basketry and other significant publications. During the late nineteenth and early twentieth centuries there was great enthusiasm for collecting Indian baskets, and several fine books that have since become classics were written then.

Books containing drawings, paintings, or photographs from earlier periods are worth searching for depictions of baskets in use, but one must keep in mind the fact that too many artists were casual in their delineation of basket forms. However, a clearly painted oval basket with domed cover, similar to the handbag version of the Nantucket

Lightship Baskets, appears in an often-reproduced unfinished water-color by the young (about nineteen) Samuel F. B. Morse, versatile inventor of the telegraph, showing his parents and their three sons in family conference.

A Winslow Homer exhibition included several paintings that displayed baskets, one an 1876 masterpiece entitled *The Two Guides.* "Old Mountain Phillips," as he was known around Keene Valley in upper New York State's Adirondacks, is shown with his young giant of a partner;[1] a large splint pack basket is visible around the bearded older man's left shoulder. A visit to the private Read Mullan Gallery of Western Art in Phoenix, Arizona, turned up a painting of a Hopi ceremonial called *Basket Dance.*

Of course, the best way to familiarize oneself with forms is through firsthand examination of documented examples in museum collections. But, with the exception of special-interest museums, such as those of Shaker or Indian artifacts, which have been more fortunate in being able to make a serious and quite successful attempt to assure authenticity, seldom can baskets be said to be well documented. So many have just "been there" a long time, and any existing catalogue cards probably bear inadequate source data. One museum staffer told me that some of their baskets were not catalogued at all, only recorded in the order of acquisition, and then merely listed in inventories of the various buildings.

Baskets were so taken for granted and cost so little that it is difficult to unearth accurate descriptions of them in estate records, where they were usually identified by function when mentioned at all. Curatorial people have been forced to round up, wherever they can, old baskets that look suitable for their exhibits. Splint baskets clearly Indian in origin are identified on one major museum's otherwise detailed accession cards as "American." Of course, they are that, but the unique or distinctive achievements of a minority can be overlooked if not marked out or differentiated in some way.

Here are museum collections with which I am familiar and can recommend as worth seeing: ROBERT ABBE MUSEUM OF STONE AGE AN-

TIQUITIES, Acadia National Park at Sieur des Monts Spring, near Bar Harbor, Maine (*Maine Indian*); THE AMERICAN MUSEUM OF NATURAL HISTORY, New York (*for Indian baskets of the Northwest Coast, Plains, and Eastern Woodlands; small Man in Africa Hall display of Afro-American baskets with connections*); APPALACHIAN MUSEUM, Berea, Kentucky; CHICAGO HISTORICAL SOCIETY (*Pioneer Life Exhibit*); COLONIAL WILLIAMSBURG, Williamsburg, Virginia (*Basketmaker's Shop*); THE HENRY FRANCIS DU PONT WINTERTHUR MUSEUM, Winterthur, Delaware; FARMERS' MUSEUM, Cooperstown, New York; FIELD MUSEUM OF NATURAL HISTORY, Chicago (*Indian collections*); THE PETER FOULGER MUSEUM OF THE NANTUCKET HISTORICAL ASSOCIATION, Nantucket, Massachusetts (*Nantucket Lightship Baskets*); HANCOCK SHAKER VILLAGE, Hancock, Massachusetts; THE HEARD MUSEUM OF ANTHROPOLOGY AND PRIMITIVE ART, Phoenix, Arizona (*Southwest Indian*); MILWAUKEE PUBLIC MUSEUM, Milwaukee, Wisconsin (*Indian collections*); MUSEUM OF AMANA HISTORY, Amana, Iowa; MUSEUM OF THE AMERICAN INDIAN, Heye Foundation, New York; MUSEUM OF THE CHEROKEE INDIAN, Cherokee, North Carolina; MUSEUM OF NEW MEXICO, Santa Fe, New Mexico (*Indian section includes a Hopi pueblo interior with various baskets*); MUSEUM OF NORTHERN ARIZONA, Flagstaff, Arizona (*Southwest Indian*); OLD STURBRIDGE VILLAGE, Sturbridge, Massachusetts; PENNSYLVANIA FARM MUSEUM OF LANDIS VALLEY, Lancaster, Pennsylvania; THE SHAKER MUSEUM, Old Chatham, New York; THE SHAKER MUSEUM, Sabbathday Lake, Poland Spring, Maine; SHELBURNE MUSEUM, INC., Shelburne, Vermont; SMITHSONIAN INSTITUTION, Washington, D.C. (*Indian collections and special crafts exhibits*).

The Farmers' Museum at Cooperstown, Hancock Shaker Village, and The Shaker Museum at Old Chatham have permanent exhibits on basketmaking. The Appalachian Museum, Museum of Amana History, and Pennsylvania Farm Museum group most of their collections. The Shelburne Museum, Old Sturbridge Village, and Winterthur scatter their baskets throughout. Most Indian collections have special basketry displays as well as other placements. When visiting larger museums, it is wise to ask the locations of standing exhibits that include baskets and whether there are any special temporary ones. In general, at restorations and reconstructions, I check out kitchens, loom rooms, barns, attics, and farm industry presentations. Dozens of other museums, restorations, and the proliferating living historical farms that I have visited have almost invariably shown some baskets, but the above twenty-odd collections are the most interesting I've found among those that are open to the public. Although some museums customarily have their entire collections on view, others keep many in storage.

Research with local historical societies may be extremely time-consuming but it can be informative and entertaining, especially if one searches in a former basket-producing area. Material from the Sandwich, New Hampshire, Historical Society, loaned in connection with my request for information about Basket Street, turned up personal bits about two weavers: Hanson Libbey, who lived on that road and was remembered for baskets said to "hold water" and bring a higher price than the ordinary run; and John Fogg, better recalled for his brow-mopping exhortations at church services.

Antiques dealers who have lived a long time in an area have seen a lot of merchandise come and go and, if attentive to baskets, can be quite helpful. New baskets often aid in identifying old forms where there has been a continuity of tradition, as in the Appalachians, so, when traveling or reading travel publications, watch for them.

Part of research should consist of observing demonstrations, either informally at the basketmaker's shop or those planned in connection with craft fairs or exhibitions. Undoubtedly the best-known basketmaking demonstrations are those by Colonial Williamsburg's two craftsmen. The foundation's film, *Basketmaking in Colonial Virginia,* is based on a demonstration by Mr. and Mrs. William Cody Cook; it is shown there frequently and is available for rental or purchase.

The reader who'd like to learn more about construction may opt to take up weaving by striking out with a book of instruction and convenient purchased materials, and going on to original designs and experimentation with all kinds of gathered plant fibers. One professional known to the writer taught himself to weave through trial-and-error preparation of splint by pounding soaked logs in the traditional Indian manner and studying and trying to copy old baskets. He also practiced techniques using commercially available reed and a craft book by Osma Gallinger Tod. Her latest volume, *Earth Basketry* (1972), includes material from previous works and pursues the collection and preparation of native fibers; another professional mentioned it as the most useful manual he knew.

Courses are not easy to locate. Short-term craft school courses encountered include one that took up "coiling, plaiting, twining, and the gathering and processing of natural materials" and another billed as "techniques of the American Indian adapted to encourage creative expression," covering basic weaving methods using wild and cultivated materials, the making of simple basketry tools, and the preparation of natural dyes. In cities with Indian concentrations, community-run organizations sometimes conduct basketry classes as a way to teach young people of their heritage. The Eastern Band of Cherokee in North Carolina participate in well-attended courses intended for professional training and conducted through a technical school by the Home Extension Service. A leading Pomo (California) feathered-basket weaver has been conducting classes attended by non-Indians.

An innovative craft being referred to by some adherents as "contemporary basketry" is attracting attention. It is most often a form of sculptural textile art that produces container shapes through a coiling technique in which core material such as hemp, unspun jute, or linen is sewn with tapestry needle and yarns and the whole sometimes ornamented with small objects. The pieces are deliberately decorative rather than utilitarian, and a whole range of possibilities in coiling and other methods are photographed in Dona Z. Meilach's *A Modern Approach to Basketry with Fibers and Grasses (Using Coiling, Twining, Weaving, Macramé, Crocheting)* (1974). Basketry is just beginning to participate in the widespread resurgence of interest several other crafts have been enjoying for some years. I hope we may see fuller appreciation of traditional baskets as well as creatively expanded uses of native fibers and dyes in forms that retain functionality.

SOURCES

Baskets are convenient and lightweight to carry home from trips. They can be found almost anywhere one travels. As a hunting territory for old baskets, New England leads for age, variety, quality, interest, and quantity. I recommend starting a list of dealers in various areas who handle baskets and visiting them when nearby or keeping in touch with them. Collector acquaintances or other dealers will often supply their names, and, of course, they should be watched for at antiques shows. Most small dealers exhibit only locally, if at all, so planning a trip to take in a few antiques shows is efficient and effective. I was surprised by the selection of baskets offered at a Massachusetts museum-town show one fall recently. Most of the collector's farm baskets will come from dealers specializing in *country antiques,* using the words loosely to mean anything rural with a little age on it, or primitives.

I am told that, if one knows where to look back in the hills, old baskets can be turned up from dealers in the Southern Highlands. I confess that I have not tried to scrounge up (anywhere) baskets from private rural owners, having had neither the time nor the temerity. And it is wise to resist the temptation to chase after a peaceful Amish farmer marketing in Middlebury or Shipshewana, Indiana, in the hope of persuading him to part with the fine old handmade baskets imagined to be hanging in his barn. He doubtless has sold any he had to the first picker-dealer who offered what seemed a good price at the time and has long been using plastic and other mass-produced containers, just like everyone else.

Outlying dealers, particularly in New England, Pennsylvania, New York, and the Midwest (get directories or lists of dealer association members wherever possible) ordinarily handle baskets when they can get them. Most small-town dwellers used to have a vegetable patch and perhaps a few chickens, as well as farm-based ancestors, so house sales yield baskets handed down in families. Farm auctions can be fruitful for those with time to attend them, but sometimes there are surprises. One of my minor fiascoes involved a small, handled willow basket that contained dried strawberry bits and seemed to be straight out of an embroidery picture, which was bid in by a dealer at a rural auction in north-central Illinois. The immediate provenance seemed right enough, but the proportions of the flaring form and fine, irregular, peeled osiers nagged at me until library research uncovered its Mexican origin.

A little study in advance of a trip can arm you with the knowledge of what to look for in the region. It is well to keep an open mind, however, because of the high mobility of antiques dealers and their merchandise, and the unreliability of too many preconceived notions. The collector might expect to find cheese baskets in the dairy state of Wisconsin, but a knowledgeable Milwaukee dealer has not. Investigation would probably indicate that the state was widely settled only after cheese production had become a factory operation rather than a farm industry.

Some florist's shops managed by collectors carry old and/or new baskets. Sources for new work include quality craft shops, especially those operated or supplied by regional guilds of artisans; museum shops like those of the Smithsonian and the Museum of the American Indian; and direct purchase from the weavers themselves. Of course, a good many basketmakers live off the beaten path, often without telephones, and are a real challenge to locate even with good directions. It is possible to arrange a specific commission, but it is preferable to stay within forms with which the worker is most familiar.

The Indian Arts and Crafts Board of the United States Department of the Interior has published two source directories, one for "Indian and Eskimo Organizations Marketing Native American Arts and Crafts" and the other for individuals, and the board has a retail Indian Craft Shop in Washington, D.C.

To continue to enjoy the well-made baskets of honest craftworkers, the collector must be willing to pay prices that offer at least a fair wage to the artisan. The decline in most areas and near-disappearance in others of skillful American Indian basketry has largely been due to switching into more remunerative employment. It is difficult to believe the number of hours spent at the arduous tasks of gathering and processing materials and weaving them into a complex basket; in the case of a superb Southwest Indian example, it may take weeks or months. Although many will say that today's young people are loath to take the time to learn a craft well, one informant noted that he knew of older people who refused to teach for fear of competition from their students.

Some materials must be purchased. In northwestern Arkansas, where splint basketmakers only recently paid four dollars for a white oak log, bidding from the railroad for crossties has pushed the price to seven dollars. Another not-unexpected problem arises when formerly functional handcraft items begin to be viewed and purchased as decorative objects. Commercial orientation, with increased emphasis on salability and probable easing of requirements for utility, may result in deteriorating quality and construction. I was once chided by a folkcraft expert for complaining of the uninspired forms and casual finishing of some very simple new Appalachian splint baskets that I had just seen. He pointed out that, although they might not "appeal" to me, the baskets did fulfill their utilitarian purposes. Of course, judgment can be passed from differing points of view.

As the early basketmaker collected and used the plant fibers that were about, so I collected from among the baskets to be found. I especially sought out and chose the most interesting, with an eye, also, to building a collection representing a wide range of forms, materials, and techniques. But I admit to being hopelessly partial to the colorful Hopi wickerwork plaques of Third Mesa and the varied baskets of the Eastern Band of Cherokee, the coiled sweet-grass Gullah baskets of South Carolina, and the elegantly simple old Shaker work. Collect those that will mean something to you, and buy for quality—beauty, craftsmanship, and honesty—all to be found in an unassuming plaited yucca-leaf sifter that smells of the desert plant and has persisted in exactly that form for over nine hundred years.

IDENTIFICATION

Any body of collectibles presents unique difficulties for the enthusiast. Determination of age and origin is really the stickiest problem in basket collecting. Few baskets come with reliable data, and condition can be indicative of use rather than age.

The movement of merchandise from one dealer to another and another is incredible. The antique basket collector's sources will be dealers, some who have long been established in a community and others who are more mobile and may be hard put to remember accurately the provenance of a particular purchase. This is of little concern to casual buyers who don't pay too dearly. Old baskets are still to be found at relatively modest cost; but the prices are escalating, and the baskets do take some searching out. While on the subject of price, let me say that one of my peeves is to be given the gratuitous advice that chances of building a quality collection of anything old for a modest figure are slight and that I should have begun around the turn of the century. I don't feel undue anguish over the fifty-cent baskets I'll never see; had I been there to collect them, I'd be long gone now.

There are in the Southern Highlands today quite elderly weavers making rib-type baskets identical to those that they have been producing since their teens and to those made by their parents and grandparents, which goes to prove the formidability of accurately dating what is a fundamental design. So many mountaineers are the descendants of immigrants from England, Scotland, and Ireland, and I have seen baskets of similar construction in nineteenth-century photographs taken in the fishing village of Newhaven, Scotland.

Sturdy wickerwork baskets have long been common in Europe and are being imported into the United States today. New coiled-straw or grass baskets are coming in from Italy, Yugoslavia, Poland, and China, usually bound with dark bark strips. The collector needs to examine such imports in order not to mistake them for their American counterparts. The differences are often subtle variations in line, proportion, binding fibers, or handles, and familiarity develops the eye for such details.

The basketmaker has been anonymous, in that it has not been customary for either individuals or families to sign their baskets. With the exception of the Nantucket Lightship Baskets, any name or set of initials appearing on one is almost invariably that of an owner. Occasionally, an original design has come to be called by the creator's name. It has been a relatively recent trend for outstanding basketmakers among the Eastern Band of Cherokee and in the Southwest to acquire national reputations, basketry having lagged behind some other crafts in this respect.

Whereas a botanist might well consider fiber classification intriguing, the average collector may be satisfied to be able to distinguish oak, ash, and hickory, the three common woods for splint, from each other. One should examine several weavers to determine the grain, which may be more noticeable or easily seen on the rougher inside. Ash splint has a less obvious grain and has some satiny sheen when smoothed. This is most apparent in black ash splintwork by Eastern Woodlands Indians that has been permitted to age gracefully through several decades of gentle handling. The parallel lines in oak are somewhat more irregular and farther apart than those in hickory, which are close and even. White oak sapwood, the part used for splints, is almost white, the heartwood being a light brown. New hickory splints are light creamy white, darkening with age to a rich, deep reddish brown. A hickory basket is heavy for its size, the splints usually thicker. A basket may incorporate two or three woods in its parts: ribs, handle, hoops, and splints.

The oldest baskets did not incorporate nails. Basketmakers prided themselves on not using machine-cut or wire nails when they became available cheaply, and some weavers do not use them even today. About the last date for hand-forged nails is 1870. Machine-cut nails— also square-headed but less irregular in head and length—were common from the 1790s to 1890, after which wire nails were used almost exclusively.[2] Copper nails having always been more expensive, their presence in an old basket is indicative of a bit more ambition on the craftworker's part, but they are seldom found. As they used various woods, so the Shakers used nails of different metals; it should be an obvious myth that the mere presence of brass nails indicates Shaker manufacture (a present-day basket factory uses them exclusively). Also untrue is Shaker attribution for so-called heart-shaped handles (see pl. 37). Although many Shaker handles were thickened (swelled to a greater thickness in the center) to make grasping easier, a device as likely to be English Colonial as Indian, they were not actually brought down to a point.

I have heard of a museum curator-collector who used his extraordinarily sensitive nose to help identify Indian baskets. A dealer told me that the man would take a basket off by itself and sniff at it. Perhaps he could then sort out the plant scents of the materials or dyes used, or the cooking odors with which it had become permeated. I do know that many sweet-grass baskets retain a fresh odor for any number of years. A trained tactile sense may be of assistance with wood or other identification.

Let us discuss the pitfalls awaiting the unwary collector. These range from "Navajo wedding baskets," which were really plain coiled baskets with the correct herringbone edge but clumsily *painted* with the appropriate star design, to "Shaker" potato-type block-stamped baskets. Shaker workmanship is so prestigious that the name has been tagged to any and all baskets that might have been Shaker-made and a good many that bear them no resemblance whatsoever. Because Shaker communities acquired design-stamped baskets from their Indian neighbors, these are all too often identified as Shaker products. I have also seen baskets with colored weavers of varying widths, an Amerindian technique, called Amish because they came out of such farm sales.

The potato-type block-stamped decoration, which superseded freehand painting and began toward the end of the eighteenth century, had been applied to broad splints; its decline came when fine splints came into universal use among Indians of the Northeast. The latest date for the technique's survival among Algonkians of southern New England is about 1890, uncertain among the Iroquois, and it lingered on in Canada in occasional use until the mid-twentieth century. Such decorations were frequently used on rectangular covered baskets, surviving lids from which have been mistakenly sold as trays. I am told that one Maine man is taking old baskets, applying color to the weavers, and adding potato-type design motifs with a Magic Marker.

All baskets that seem to be Indian in manufacture are not. A non-Indian Michigan-born woman remembers that she and her classmates learned to weave splint baskets from a tribeswoman in the northern part of that state as recently as the midpoint of this century. A publication called *The Basket: The Journal of the Basket Fraternity of Lovers of Indian Baskets and Other Good Things,* a quarterly published in Pasadena, at least during 1903 and 1904, include an advertisement for "actual working designs drawn from the collections of George Wharton James and others, with full particulars for the weaver, showing the number of coils of weave, colors, design, significance, size, etc. (so that) any person may succeed in making a good basket using these model designs." Photographs of successful attempts were run in this quarterly.

CONDITION AND CARE

The "bewares" concerning condition include the reminder to look for sloppy repairs, wired rims, weavers or rim binding replaced with such inappropriate materials as chair caning, missing (examine the rim carefully for gaps or remaining ends) or loose handles. Of course, the collector should walk away from wrecks of baskets, but a few broken splints are not serious or normally avoidable. A Maine dealer who handles a good many baskets knows a young man who does a fine job of even difficult repairs. However, securing proper repairs will likely prove an insurmountable obstacle for the typical collector, so buy only baskets that are acceptable as they are. New baskets are sometimes carelessly put together, the handles thin and weak, misshapen, or attached so poorly that they will give way easily; splints may not be well scraped and smoothed, either to save time or because the weaver cannot obtain good timber.

A collector who limits himself to perfect, immaculately cleaned old specimens misses the softened appearance that comes with years of everyday service. But basketry can be fairly readily destroyed by water, heat, and vermin. A certain minimum care, such as regular cleaning and avoiding placement in cooking areas where a greasy film might accumulate, is essential. When bringing in a new basket, any dried-on bits of food should be thoroughly removed, to avoid attracting insects. Encrusted soil is far better brushed away than hosed off, for even solid-looking old wicker baskets can be brittle. A dealer I met cleans very dirty baskets with a sponge or brush dipped into soapsuds and follows with a sponge rinse. I have seen photographs of archaeological team members removing the debris of centuries with a shampoo hosing on a well-drained surface, and one expert on Indian baskets recommends washing in a tub of lukewarm water with mild soap, thorough rinsing, and drying out of direct sunlight.[3]

Soaking can quickly cause dry baskets to swell and soften, leading to warping or splitting when handled. I think that the whole point is to wet a basket as little as possible. In general, absolute cleanliness isn't worth risking damage. Think in terms of freshening a basket and restoring humidity, which can usually be accomplished with a gentle brushing and a wipe with a moist cloth or perhaps a short period in a steamy room. Some collectors rely on an occasional rinse. A Chitimacha basketweaver who owns several river-cane baskets fifty to two hundred years old says that she rinses them about once a year, believing it helps to preserve the fiber. Although basketry shouldn't be kept damp, some humidity is essential to keep the fibers pliant. In a northern climate, a humidifier operating during the winter eliminates the problem of hot, drying blasts of forced air.

It may seem incongruous to be warned of the dangers of a basket's drying out, when we know that basketry nine thousand years old has been recovered in the desert of the American Southwest. The longevity of these pieces was due to particularly fortunate conditions and burial in dry sand, an excellent preservative. Fibers cannot long survive exposure in an open site, but constantly wet clay or mud has also been known to seal off air so effectively as to prevent attack by bacteria or fungi for a number of centuries.

Keeping a basket dust- and vermin-free and providing enough humidity for it to stay flexible may be all that is needed to keep it in good condition. However, some museums use a cleaning and preservative formula of half *boiled* linseed oil and half turpentine, lightly applied and rubbed down thoroughly. To clean a basket of accumulated grime, some antiques dealers substitute white vinegar for half of the turpentine portion. Coiled-straw baskets should only be dry-brushed or lightly wiped with a damp cloth.

Silicone spraying for a shiny effect is to be deplored. Perhaps the worst thing that can happen to a basket is to be shellacked, lacquered, or varnished. I am a purist and dislike the artificial appearance, but even more serious is the fact that coating the surface seals in the fibers and blocks absorption of vital moisture from the air.

Dealers have told me how they remove paint or glaze from baskets, and these techniques involve such possibilities as throwing the baskets into a tub of hot water to which some ammonia has been added; rubbing with a cloth soaked in wood alcohol (thorough drying and steaming should follow the use of solvents); or, if the paint is only in accidental spatters or drips, a common finding, rubbing with steel wool or sandpaper or scraping with a pocketknife. With the exception of the last-mentioned, I haven't tried these myself. I consider it safer— and a statement of protest—to avoid purchasing baskets that have been slathered with paint, shellac, or varnish. I do not refer to nineteenth-century baskets colored with homemade paints of the period,

FIGURE 17. Country cupboard providing good display and storage for a basket collection. This particular cabinet is of pine, made in Wales or elsewhere in England about 1830. The recessed top is handy for bulky baskets, and the enclosed bottom can serve to hide less-sightly contents.

presumably by owners who acquired them in natural wood and used up a little leftover paint that way; they should be left untouched.

Fungi and some twenty or thirty varieties of termites and wood beetles attack plant fibers. Otis T. Mason, in "Directions for Collectors of American Basketry," [4] recommends poisoning baskets—his item has the chemistry. But the smell of a freshly poisoned basket is hard to live with, and it can't be used to hold edibles. (An interesting aside is that I was well into this article before I realized that "American basketry" meant only American Indian basketry to Mr. Mason.) Also, any wet chemical treatment, including an antimildew or insect spray, may leave a white residue or otherwise discolor the fiber. Simple airing will eliminate an unpleasant musty odor. Confinement with paradichlorobenzene crystals, commonly used against moths, will kill insects, but the nuggets should not be left in contact with the baskets.

The reader is cautioned to handle antique baskets carefully, lifting with both hands cupping the bottom—never dragging, or forcing the piece into tight spaces—and to remember that handles and rims are vulnerable to splitting when pressured.

Baskets are pale and rather too fresh looking when new, but artificially aging a basket by hanging it outdoors to weather is disapproved and can be quite damaging. Exposure to normal inside light darkens them; they do begin to mellow within a few months, even within a cabinet.

DISPLAY AND USE

I like to mass or at least group most of my baskets and scatter others through the house in appropriate functional or decorative placements.

FIGURE 18. Basket "tree." Really an old footed wash-drying rack with three tiers, each with a dozen fold-away arms. This one had to be stripped of several layers of chipped white paint. Popular with antiques dealers (who can easily take them along to shows) for holding textiles and baskets, they are not easily come by. H. 5½′; W. top tier 28″; W. other two 32″.

A country cupboard (fig. 17) is a perfect piece of furniture; the top comes in handy for bulky baskets, and an enclosed bottom hides less slightly study materials. Many collectors like to hang baskets from small hooks in the ceiling, pegs on exposed beams, or a "tree." A choice basket tree is a footed, vertical wooden wash-drying rack with fold-away arms that swing out at several heights—great for display, but it takes some searching to get one (fig. 18).

A dealer-collector I know hangs smaller baskets from a row of Shaker pegs around the room. A soffit, ledge, or high shelf presents an ideal display area for baskets mixed with pottery and other suitable collectibles. There is a whole range of possibilities in wall-mounted or ceiling-hung racks with hooks. These include old butchers', meat, or game racks. A fine English example of the last-named was seen at an antiques show; it had a carved wooden backplate sixty-four-inches long, from which hung the fifteen original iron hooks, and dated from about 1800. A circa 1865 Dutch solid brass wall coat rack forty-nine-inches long had ten movable hooks, and additional baskets could be hung from the ends of the rods. An easy acquisition is a corn dryer (see the homemade one in fig. 19), whose prongs formerly impaled ears of seed corn.

A sun porch with wicker or primitive furnishings is an ideal place for a basket feature. The ceiling must be high enough so that any hanging baskets and tall guests' heads do not collide. I like the look of including bunches of dried herbs and flowers hung from the rafters.

A few notes of caution: Be certain that the handles are strong enough, and don't load weakened old baskets with books, dishes, or other heavy things and then try to hang them or move them about. Baskets are also vulnerable to being stabbed with sharp objects, and, once a weaver is broken, use leads to other breaks. Wall-mounted

FIGURE 19. Baskets and colored ears hung on a corn dryer: c. 1870–1880. This homemade wooden piece once impaled eighteen seed ears on its prongs. The type is much less common than the flat ten-prong cast-iron versions subsequently made in small-town iron forges or by blacksmiths.

FIGURE 20. Dried plant materials arranged in suitable basket forms. The arrangement need not be elaborate, perhaps simply a bunch of statice or a handful of field grasses like foxtail. In groupings, I like most of the containers to be filled with a single kind of dried stuff, but some mixes and even a few feathers add variety.

installations for shallow baskets like cheese baskets can be accomplished with nails or L-hooks, but they should be hung from a sturdy part of the basket rather than through an existing break.

I have several good-sized Gullah baskets sitting together on a bit of floor space between scatter rugs and out of the traffic pattern so they can't be stepped onto, and I find that people tend to examine such a like group more closely. I have heard of one collector who piles a heap of baskets in one corner, with striking effect. Another suggestion is to stack similar covered baskets that don't have handles at the top—potato-stamped baskets in graduated sizes are fine—into a tower.

Baskets make most attractive plant or flower holders, lined, of course, with saucers or other watertight containers deep enough to avoid having an overflow sop the basket or run out onto the floor or tabletop. They are convenient as desk trays, for fruit or snacks, they provide storage for linens and games or, like a sewing basket, can be put to their intended purposes about the home. Outdoors people order pack baskets; hobbyists use baskets to display collections of shells or old marbles; picnickers carry lunches in hampers. Wall baskets can hold mail or craft supplies. Bottle, jar, or bowl forms look right for dried arrangements (fig. 20).

Baskets contribute texture, color, warmth, interest—and perhaps a focal point—to an interior that offers a comforting "sense of shelter." They are fun to collect, represent a relatively modest investment, and fit in with the nostalgia for a simpler time that is implicit in our rediscovered concern with the roots and handcrafts of the American heritage. Our humble farm and household baskets, produced for utility with an only-sometimes intent to achieve beauty, too, are appealing symbols of our mostly past rural life.

NOTES

1. Jean Gould, *Winslow Homer, A Portrait* (New York: Dodd, Mead & Company, 1962), p. 132.
2. Raymond F. Yates, *Antique Fakes and Their Detection* (New York: Gramercy Publishing Company, a division of Crown Publishers, Inc., by arrangement with Harper & Row, Publishers, 1950), pp. 94–95.
3. Dr. Frank W. Lamb, *Indian Baskets of North America* (Riverside, Calif.: Riverside Museum Press, 1972), p. 2.
4. Otis T. Mason, "Directions for Collectors of American Basketry," *Bulletin of the United States National Museum*, No. 39, Pt. P. (Washington, D.C.: Government Printing Office, 1902).

Gallery of Baskets

PLATE 1. Winnowing fan: early nineteenth century. After flailing, grain was scooped up and tossed into the air, the wind blowing away the chaff and the grain dropping back into the basket or falling to the ground or barn floor or into another basket. The man who could use this fan had to have quite an armspread. L. 31″; W. 35″; D. 9½″. Photograph courtesy the Chicago Historical Society.

PLATE 2. Splint basket with movable handle pinned to wedge-shaped sockets: 1800–1850. The pegs have large, square nutlike heads, and the construction is similar to that found in old wooden buckets. The wood is a white oak, quite possibly swamp chestnut oak or basket oak. O.H. 17½″; Diam. 16½″. Photograph courtesy The Henry Francis du Pont Winterthur Museum, Winterthur, Delaware.

PLATE 3. Splintwork laundry/wash basket from the Northeast: late nineteenth or early twentieth century. The bottom (seen at upper left in plate 32, where it is hanging near a display of cheese baskets) is open checkerwork, employed where drainage is needed or for air circulation, as in fruit-drying trays. The top appears ovoid with flattened ends because of the insertion of a pair of heavy handles between the hoops of the double rim. A similar basket is made today by a descendant of a several-generations basketmaking family in the Taghkanic Hills of New York State. O.II. 13"; Outside rim 19¾" x 18".

PLATE 4. Four-legged basket, probably for rinsing wool: nineteenth century. Splint with openwork bottom. After cleansing in a hot solution, raw wool was fresh-water rinsed and drained in baskets set up on legs. The only other four-legged basket I have examined was a very sturdy, large oblong with solid splint bottom; perhaps its legs were intended simply to keep the contents up off a damp floor. O.H. 19½"; Diam. 21"; Legs 3". Photograph courtesy the New York State Historical Association, Cooperstown, New York.

PLATE 5. Work/sewing/mending/ darning baskets. The carefully woven nineteenth-century example (at left) resembles one at The Shaker Museum at Old Chatham, New York, except that it does not have a cross-bound rim, the handles are more simply carved, and the ribs are not heavier than the weavers. Some of these forms seem to have been made in nests. The openwork specimen (at right), probably late nineteenth century, is one variant of a design that has existed here since Colonial days, making it extremely difficult to date. Usually of willow, some were made of honeysuckle vine after its introduction into the Southeast in the later nineteenth century. Those with more open spaces were lined to prevent the escape of small sewing items. Nowadays, such baskets are thought of as fruit holders for the table. One huge willow example actually had a 30″ diameter, perhaps intended as a showpiece for a basketmaker's shop. Left: O.H. 5¾″; Diam. 14¾″. Right: D. 4¾″; Diam. 12½″.

PLATE 6. Individual covered lunch baskets (probable use): both probably later nineteenth century. The lid and bottom of the Northeast ash basket (at right) are of identical checkerwork, the cover bound to the rim along one side. A perfect example of the variations on a theme often noticed in basketry—of two similar pieces examined, one (at The Shaker Museum at Old Chatham, New York) had a slotted cover that slid up on the handle in the manner of feather baskets, and the other had a double-hinged lid. The basket (at left) of imported cane over heavy wood-splint ribs individually wired to splints forming the rim and base circumference bears a metal nameplate on which the "MR." has been altered to "MRS.," wire fastenings, and shreds of a paper lining. The bottom, of wood splints and rattan bound to a heavy wire rectangle, was made separately and is wired to the wide base band. From the mid-South, a thick coat of sooty grime on the top suggested service in a rail yard, mill, or mine. Left: O.H. 8"; L. 9½"; W. 5½". Right: O.H. 11¼"; L. 13½"; W. 8½".

PLATE 7. Covered oval baskets with pair of braided swing handles passing over the top: mid- to late nineteenth century. Wickerwork. A purse basket or woman's workbasket similar to that in the right foreground is in the collection of The Shaker Museum at Old Chatham, New York, where it is identified as Shaker-made but exhibiting European design influence. Large ones like that at the rear, fifteen-plus inches long, served as family lunch baskets for churchgoing and social gatherings. They seem to have been popular with German families and are sometimes called Amish, although they probably would once have been considered too fancy for those strict people. The example at the left just may have come out of the China Trade, as have known examples of paler fibers and colored bands in similar oval or round forms.

PLATE 8. Wickerwork market baskets, peeled osiers. Such good-sized handled baskets served in a dual capacity, not only taking small farm products to market and purchases home, but gathering from the family vegetable patch. An unpretentious Victorian basket (at right) of clean lines and good proportions, dating in the 1870s. O.H. 15¼"; L. 18½"; W. 13". A three-rod weave in a basket (at left) collected in Cedarburg, Wisconsin, and believed to have been locally manufactured early in this century. O.H. 12¼"; L. 19½"; W. 12". With both baskets, the ends of the willow rods in the twisted handles tie into the rim.

PLATE 9. Cutflower/cutting basket: c. late nineteenth century. (The form is known in the Ozarks as a sandwich basket.) This well-made white oak-splint piece for gathering flowers or herbs from the garden has been dark-stained somewhere along the way. Decorative and ever popular for a center-piece display of fruit or autumn arrangements of gourds, squashes, and corn, large ones such as this also function as magazine baskets, and, because they tend to rock, are sometimes stabilized with a pair of cleats. O.H. 14½"; L. 20¾"; W. 16¾".

PLATE 10. Wood/firewood/log/chip/kindling carriers and storage baskets. Three splint forms are common. The most prevalent is shown (at right) in an example probably from the latter half of the nineteenth century. O.H. 14½"; L. 25½"; W. 17½". A semicircular-sided version is represented by this 16½" nailed-rim specimen (at left), made in reduced size either as a sample or intended for a child's use; the form is known to have been woven by at least one Southern Highlands artisan into the 1960s. A third form has perpendicular rectangular sides and is being made today by the Eastern Band of Cherokee in North Carolina of white oak splint.

PLATE 11. Collection of miniature baskets. Papago coiled bowl (lower center) of split yucca leaf in natural colors. A white oak-splint and a honeysuckle vine basket (center) by the Cherokee of North Carolina. Two honeysuckle vine baskets and a 3″-long white oak-splint rib-type (left) from elsewhere in the Southern Highlands. Passamaquoddy thimble case (lower right) of ash splint and sweet grass. A fine handled, covered basket (upper right) of undetermined origin. All but the last were collected new in their respective regions in 1973 and 1974.

PLATE 12. New England Algonkian freehand-painted berry-picking basket: early to mid-nineteenth century. Broad black ash splints and usual checkerwork square bottom. Note that every other rib is turned over the rim (the alternates are cut off), narrowed to a point, and tucked under a weaver, a procedure called *hemming*. The casual decoration may have been applied with a frayed twig dipped into berry juice. The Mohegan were known to use a bundle of matchsticks tied in a cluster to produce a pattern of dots, a technique related to block-stamping (pl. 13). O.H. 10¼"; Diam. 8¼".

PLATE 13. Algonkian (or possibly Iroquoian) covered basket with "potato"-type stamped designs: 1800–1825. Solid-colored ribs alternately red and black, stamping in black. Algonkian and some Iroquoian tribes, who may have adopted the method through Algonkian influence, carved a piece of vegetable, soft wood, or other material with a simple raised motif, dipped it into plant stain, and applied it to wide weavers and occasionally to ribs. The decorative technique had its precursor in freehand painting. This fine example bears a legend on the bottom in late nineteenth-century script: "Aunt Mary Hoyt's Bonnet Basket." Algonkians almost surely first wove square or rectangular baskets, easier to make and less space-consuming. Such round covered baskets were intended for white customers' use, for clothing storage, replacing hatboxes and bandboxes, and were, for example, more common in Maine than trunks for coach or packet travel. H. 10½"; Diam. 14⅜". Photograph courtesy The Henry Francis du Pont Winterthur Museum, Winterthur, Delaware.

PLATE 14. New ash-splint utility baskets by Maine weavers of Algonkian heritage. A smaller version of the Aroostook County potato basket (left foreground), usually half-bushel capacity to accommodate the strength of children, who represent most of the pickers. Larger ones have a kind of casual base border consisting of a loosely twisting splint. Rough brown (black) ash by an elderly man descended from various tribal stocks, born and living on the Penobscot Reservation on Indian Island, Old Town. (Clockwise) Rough brown ash Passamaquoddy fisherman's scale basket, a long-time standby; about 18½″ overall height and diameter. Double pie basket with separate

dome to be slipped in to separate the pies, by Frances Richard of Perry, a
Passamaquoddy location. Handled rib-type of white ash (right foreground)
by a Malecite who came from Canada as an infant and married a man of
Penobscot blood. The American Museum of Natural History, New York,
identifies such a basket as Penobscot; they are also being produced by
Mohawks (one of the Iroquois Six Nations) of Canada. Although this and
the double pie basket are attractive enough to be called decorative, they are
included here as intended for utility and left undecorated.

PLATE 15. Decorated baskets from tribes of the Northeast. Where coloration is added, synthetic dyes are used. New covered trinket basket (left end) of ash splint and sweet grass by a skillful Passamaquoddy weaver; the decorative overlay technique of curlicue is called *curly* among them and the Penobscots (where one elderly woman practices it). Older "curly-bowl" (to its right) of uncertain tribal origin. Modest "potato"-type stamped basket (left rear) from around the turn of the century; practiced by Algonkians and the Iroquois, the technique reached as far west as Wisconsin. Shallow two-handled ash basket (rear center) with every other rib indigo-painted and a few indigo-soaked weavers; it would date from the 1920s or 1930s. New

ash-splint and sweet-grass covered basket (right rear) by Irene Newell of Princeton, Maine; such decorative baskets are more recent among the Passamaquoddy than their durable utility baskets. Flatbaskets, such as this (right end) 9″-diameter example of ash splint and braided sweet grass are called, have been made by various tribes of the Northeast; it is perhaps fifty years old. The small basket (front center) with chain pattern on top is also a new Passamaquoddy piece. (Above it) Mohawk splint-and-sweet-grass basket. At least two other Iroquoian tribes, the Oneida and the Seneca, are producing splintwork. The square (left center) is a new Penobscot handkerchief box.

PLATE 16. Baskets from tribes of the western Great Lakes region: earlier twentieth century. (Rear, left to right) Potawatomi (an Algonkian tribe of Michigan and Wisconsin) rib-type of unpeeled willow; basket with incurved sides collected in Michigan, splints dyed in bright synthetic colors; handled basket (others have two swing handles crossing over) of the sort sold from roadside stands in Wisconsin in the 1920s and 1930s. (Foreground, left to right) Square ornamental basket with overlay bands of projecting points, perhaps sold as an Easter basket, Ohio Algonkian; square bottom-to-round serrated-edge tray of plaited birchbark, a much-used material around the Great Lakes, but the basket's specific origin is unknown; and a covered jar-shape with curlicue, another from the formerly prolific Ohio Algonkians. Three would have been produced strictly for sale: the Easter basket, the covered jar-shape, and the basket with incurved sides (O.H. 14¾"; L. 20¾"; W. 12½").

PLATE 17. Covered picnic hamper, western Great Lakes Indian-made for sale in northern Wisconsin or northern Michigan (it closely resembles a new Winnebago example), black ash splint and synthetic dyes of red and green with a brown stain that may be vegetal, perhaps 30 years old. The presence of colored and varied-width weavers and the lines—slightly flaring sides, with straight shoulder sloping to the rim (a shape also found on undecorated baskets)— indicate Indian manufacture. The unique treatment of the ends of the movable handles—they are tapered and bent back through one hole and terminate in another—is known to the Cherokee of North Carolina as well. The pinwheel decorations on top are a form of curlicue. H. 11½″; L. 20″; W. 15″.

PLATE 18. Contemporary baskets from the Eastern Band of Cherokee in North Carolina, incorporating the three fibers used: river cane (center), honeysuckle vine over white oak ribs (right), and white oak splint (left). Dyes are homemade vegetal. The square-to-round underarm burden basket (rear, left of center), twilled in river-cane weave, is by Agnes Welch. The shallow doubleweave basket of river cane (center) by Eva Wolfe represents a revived technique involving the simultaneous weaving of one basket inside another and results in a different pattern inside and out. The undeco-

rated basket (left center) is a fishbasket, a creel purposely made small to remind the angler to catch no more than needed. The dark bands in the 12¾" high honeysuckle vine wastebasket (rear right) are a distinctive deep purplish black-brown stain made from walnut root. The canoe-shaped and small round open baskets are for fruit. The small sewing basket with carefully fitted cover, the most popular honeysuckle vine form, is by Lucy N. George. Each of the weavers named has been honored with an individual exhibition of her work at Cherokee, North Carolina.

PLATE 19. Southern Woodlands Indian baskets. The baskets in this plate illustrate the difficulty of obtaining accurate provenance information, for the author has had to supply new attributions. (Left) Recent Choctaw (probably) cow-nose basket of cane-splint that has to be hung. A heart shape—similar baskets are pointed at the bottom—indicates a gift that comes "from the heart." Purchased from a reliable shop specializing in quality new Indian arts, it had been identified in their source records as Apache. O.H. 14¾"; L. 12¾"; W. 7¾". (Center) Coiled long-leaf pine-needle vase said to have been brought from Florida earlier in this century, which would indicate probable origin with the Seminoles, who do coiled work. H. 4½"; Diam. 6". (Right) Cane-splint handled basket that was identified as Chitimacha, c. 1925, but is more likely Cherokee, judging from the inner hickory bark wrapping of one of the double rims. O.H. 13½"; L. 11¾"; W. 8½".

PLATE 20. Chitimacha sewing basket in polychrome. Uses synthetic dyes of black, red, and yellow; twilled of native cane peeled four times with the teeth and hands. Made by the Stouffs of Jeanerette, Louisiana, this small tribe's only active weavers, to fill a 1974 commission. Their baskets are based on models 50 to 200 years old; this is identical to one included in plate 133 of "a fine collection of old Chetimacha baskets" shown in Otis Tufton Mason's "Aboriginal American Basketry" (see Selected Bibliography), published in 1902. The famed Chitimacha basketry is distinctive for execution of curvilinear patterns within a geometric weave of narrow splints. A usual form was a covered oblong basket that served a mortuary function or held small personal objects. H. 5"; Diam. 10".

PLATE 21. Makah *wabbit* basket made of cedar bark and grasses, with motifs in aniline dyes of purple, green, and red. From a tribe of the Nootka group centered at Neah Bay on Washington's Olympic Peninsula. Made to fill a commission in 1974. Twill-plaited bottom and wrapped twining, which is most easily seen in the pebbled-looking background of the wide decorative overlay band. In the wrap-twine technique, two stiff elements, a horizontal and a vertical, are held together by a flexible weft. Pictorial designs are common. These represent the wolf, a powerful totem; a whale; and a whaling boat with harpooner poised to strike. The only basket the Makahs use themselves, it carries the family's dishes to potlatches and brings home the *wabbit* (leftovers). A few elderly women weave for sale, usually in response to a request and mostly during the rainy winters. O.H. 13"; Diam. 11¾".

PLATE 22. Amerindian baskets of the Southwest. All were collected new in 1973. (Rear left) Hopi corn sifter of twilled split yucca leaf, a thousand-year-old design called a ring basket for its hoop rim. (Rear center) Hopi sumac and rabbit brush plaque or tray in the whirlwind pattern, native and synthetic dyes. (Rear right) Navajo coiled "wedding" basket in white, black, and reddish-brown, also a ceremonial bowl for ingredients used by the

shaman during healing and other rituals, and it is sometimes inverted to function as a drum. (Front right) Santo Domingo (a Rio Grande pueblo) openwork wicker basket of willow rods; shallower versions were once woven to fit rounded-bottom cooking pots, which were stabilized when in use for food storage by resting them in the baskets. (Front center) Hopi *piki* (paper-thin corn bread) tray with wickerwork border. L. 18¾"; W. 14".

PLATE 23. New England wood-bottomed basket with movable handle attached with rivet and washer. This is a cruder relative of the Nantucket Lightship Basket, with ribs inserted firmly into a groove sawed around the edge of the handmade base. A knowledgeable antiques dealer who offered a similar basket considered hers to be from about 1850, judging from the way it was made and the nails used, and stated that they are known in New England as New Hampshire baskets and forerunners of the Nantucket Lightship Baskets. D. 8″; Diam. 9½″.

PLATE 24. Kettle-shaped New England egg basket with bail handle: mid-nineteenth century. Ash splint. As with many baskets intended for eggs or other fragile contents, the bottom has a raised center. This cuts down breakage or bruising by minimizing rolling about of rounded items and permits the slightly flaring sides to carry part of the weight, rather than having the whole load bearing down heavily at the middle. In the double-spider-web base, ribs (there are 33) are alternately carried to the inside or the outside with a little space between the sets, resulting in a kind of false bottom (which I've heard called a "kickup") to lend strength and protection. The movable handle and bows are carefully carved, and the whole construction is well conceived and executed. The symmetrical shape indicates it was woven over a mold. This basket is surprisingly flexible when rotated back and forth with the hands. H. with handle up 14¾″; D. 8¾″; Diam. 11¾″.

PLATE 25. Pigeon basket, for transporting live wild passenger pigeons: nineteenth century. Usual ovoid mouth and rigid handle. Such baskets carried birds used as decoys for netting wild flocks or for target practice. O.H. 21½″; Diam. 19″. Photograph courtesy the New York State Historical Association, Cooperstown, New York.

PLATE 26. Bottle-shaped splint basket: New England, nineteenth century. The ovoid mouth indicates it may have been a pigeon basket, in which case it originally would have had a cover. Other possible uses have been advanced: to carry a chicken to market head down; to contain the head of a live goose while being plucked upside down (they bite); or as a bottle, i.e., woven over one. O.H. 14¼"; Diam. 8". Photograph courtesy Lawrence E. King, Monroe Center, Illinois.

PLATE 27. Two-tiered checker-work basket from the Northeast: mid- to late nineteenth century. Black ash, probably Algonkian-made for sale as a picnic or storage basket. Photograph courtesy Kelter-Malcé Antiques, New York.

PLATE 28. Square-bottom-to-round-mouthed New England hickory-splint basket: mid-nineteenth century. The base is plaited in varied twill, over-one-under-three pattern in one direction and simple plaiting (over-one-under-one) in the other, the remaining ribs cut off and tucked in just after passing the bottom, half on each of the two opposite sides. A basket that has ruder New England native antecedents, its moderate size was convenient for small gathering chores and kitchen storage. O.H. 11½″; Diam. 10¾″.

PLATE 29. Tall, covered storage hamper: early to mid-nineteenth century. Oak(?) splint. Similar forms often have a pair of sturdy hand-carved handles at the sides (see pl. 70), rather than these of thin splint. H. 27"; Diam. 23"; Sq. base 14". Photograph courtesy Shelburne Museum, Inc., Shelburne, Vermont. John M. Miller, photographer.

PLATE 30. Bell-shaped Loom Room storage basket: probably mid-nineteenth century. In weaving exhibit at Shelburne Museum, oak handles and hickory(?) splint. This example bells out at the bottom; the narrower mouth is a device to keep the contents from blowing or spilling out, as in some berry-picking baskets. H. 13″; Diam. 17″. Photograph courtesy Shelburne Museum, Inc., Shelburne, Vermont.

PLATE 31. Tall, slender splint basket with three small handles and openwork bottom: nineteenth century. Its purpose is uncertain. H. 23″; Diam. top 9¾″; Sq. base 5½″. Photograph courtesy Old Sturbridge Village, Sturbridge, Massachusetts.

PLATE 32. Cheese curd baskets/ cheese baskets/cheese drainers, also known, less accurately, as cheese strainers or sieves. This dealer's display at a Midwestern antiques show includes a variety of shapes and sizes of baskets and hexagonal openwork weave. The smallest baskets were probably used instead for light kitchen food-storage duties, and a Shaker egg basket in the weave, which was also known to Eastern Woodlands Indians, is shown in plate 45. Cheese curd baskets were lined with cloth, filled with fresh curds, and set over vats that caught the dripping whey. They appear to have been a New England specialty. The large basket with risers (parallel cleats) across the bottom (D. 6¾″; Diam. 23½″) may be Shaker from the second quarter of the nineteenth century. Most of the others probably date from later in the century. (Note: The square-bottomed laundry basket which is hanging at the upper left, is shown in pl. 3.) Photograph courtesy Betty Sterling, Brainstorm Farm Antiques, Randolph, Vermont.

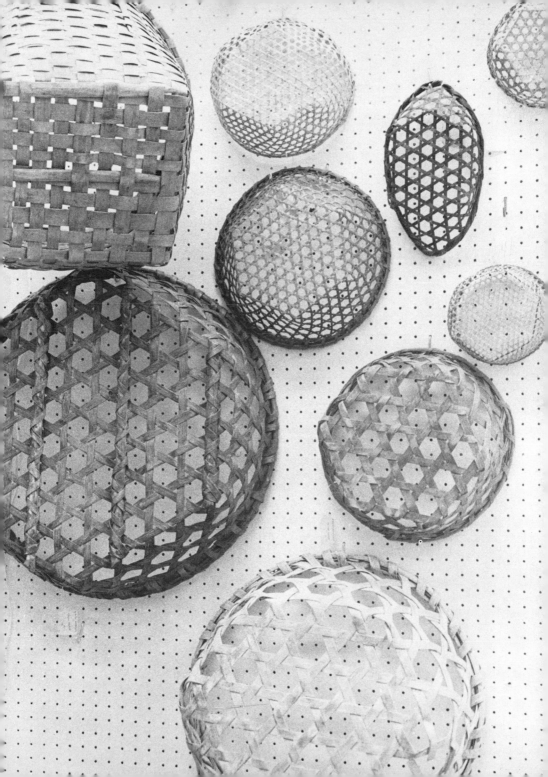

PLATE 33. Small, wickerwork, covered gathering basket. Domed top attached by loop, with a second loop for convenience in lifting lid; peeled willow rods. The dealer recalled seeing many of these hanging in barns and believed that they had been used to gather peas and such for the family table. Although I have never seen another identical to it, a similar-looking covered basket but in a much larger oval shape was dated by a long-time Vermont dealer as about 1880 to 1890. He pointed out, also, that wicker baskets came after splint baskets in that area. O.H. 10¼″; Diam. 8½″.

PLATE 34. New England ash-splint feather basket: probably late nineteenth century. In this form, the cover does not come off but is slotted to slide up on the rigid handle. This permitted the plucker of dead chickens or live geese to hold the bird with one hand and to lift the lid with the side of the hand clutching the feathers, then stuffing them in and letting the cover drop back into place to keep the fluffy goods from blowing away. Many feather-type baskets are encountered, so the form was obviously popular, even though lots of them are too small to have been practical for that purpose. O.H. 11¾"; Diam. 9".

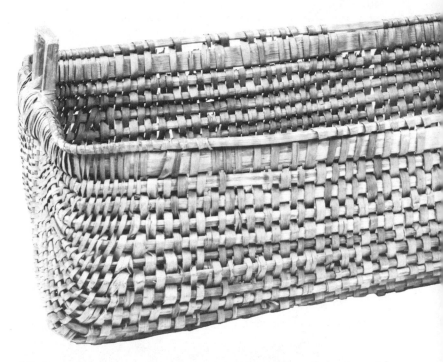

PLATE 35. Large hamper of rib-type construction: nineteenth century. The high square handles at either end do not extend down into or outside the basket but are heavily bound to the rim. O.H. 16½″; L. 39″; W. 22.″ Photograph courtesy Old Sturbridge Village, Sturbridge, Massachusetts.

PLATE 36. New England shallow oblong basket with plaited band across the rim: probably second half of the nineteenth century. The purpose of the band is unknown. There is no sign that a double-hinged lid was ever attached, but the band may have supported a separate cover or kept a cloth protecting prepared food from falling in on it. O.H. 9″; L. 16″; W. 9½″. Photograph courtesy Lawrence E. King, Monroe Center, Illinois.

PLATE 37. Two handled small-fruit gathering basket: second half of the nineteenth century. Although the size and shape might suggest that this had been intended as a wastebasket, the openwork bottom would not have been practical for that purpose. This basket has the so-called heart-shaped handles, which refers to the carving of the inside (underside) to a pointed protrusion at the center and curving up and out to the sides, the lines suggesting the top of a heart. It is more noticeable in some other specimens (see the basket at left on top of the cabinet in fig. 17) and is often found in undecorated but well-made baskets that appear to have been produced by Indian weavers in the Northeast. O.H. 13¼"; Diam. 12".

PLATE 38. Unusual carved-wood handle on a rectangular splint basket, formerly with double-hinged lid. The only example I've seen where the handle has been carved to look as if it had been turned on a lathe. The handle is carefully fitted and proportioned to the basket. One suspects its maker was a woodworker—carpenter, cooper, or cabinetmaker—turned basketmaker, probably second half of the nineteenth century. O.H. 12"; L. 21"; W. 13". Photograph courtesy Helga Photo Studio, Inc., New York.

PLATE 39. New Hampshire farm basket with out-curved sides, probably made shortly before the turn of the century. Sturdily constructed for heavy gathering use, the openwork of the square checker-plaited bottom may have been intended to permit draining when root vegetables were rinsed off in the basket and provided air circulation during their storage. Alternate ribs are bent over at the rim and tucked in on the inside, a detail reminiscent of Indian work. O.H. 17¾"; Diam. 16½".

PLATE 40. Mid-twentieth-century splint baskets of the Northeast. (Left) Covered pie basket with nailed rim and metal fittings and pair of movable handles—this for a single pie, but deeper baskets for two pies come with a tray on legs to separate them, which can be removed in order to carry a two-layer cake. The original owner (several previous owners wrote their names on the top) bought this ash-splint basket perhaps twenty years ago from a New Hampshire basket factory that is still making them. D. 5″; L.

13¼″; W. 12¾″. (Center) New oak-splint mail basket with cross-bound rim, by Elizabeth Proper of New York State. The handle is for hanging it on the wall, but the basket can stand, too. O.H. 9¾″; L. 8¾″; W. 6½″. (Right) Ash-splint egg basket with raised center and rigid handle. One of several common basket forms, similar examples were included in a National Rural Arts Exhibition held in Washington under government auspices in 1937. O.H. 13¼″; Diam. at handles 13¼″–14″.

PLATE 41. New set of four small nesting baskets, all but one with swing handles, white oak splint. Nests of baskets were once common, but most have become separated over the years. The assorted sizes were convenient for various tasks, and a set saved space. These (from one-egg to six-egg capacity) are by Elizabeth Proper, a fourth-generation prolific basketmaker living in the Taghkanic Hills of Columbia County, New York. Largest basket: D. 4"; Diam. 7½".

PLATE 42. Splint baskets at The Shaker Museum, Old Chatham, New York. The well-woven, round-mouthed, rigid-handled sort of baskets that one associates with the Shakers. This group was especially selected to illustrate a variety of bases and handles. It includes a feather-type, in which the cover does not come off but is slotted to slide up on the handle. Various woods were used by the Shakers, especially ash and hickory, and baskets were almost invariably woven over molds. The baskets are believed to have been made at Watervliet or New Lebanon (Mount Lebanon, both New York) and are presumed to date from around the mid-nineteenth century but cannot be more definitely dated, except for that at the right rear; it is marked 1832 on the handle and is 16¾" in overall height. Photograph courtesy The Shaker Museum, Old Chatham, New York.

PLATE 43. Shaker oblong market baskets: probably mid-nineteenth century. These two represent another well-known Shaker form. (Opposite, top) O.H. 15¼"; L. 17½"; W. 12¾". (Opposite, bottom) O.H. 16¼". Photographs courtesy The Shaker Museum, Old Chatham, New York.

PLATE 44. Shaker Loom Room hamper: mid-nineteenth century. Ash splint. From North Church Family, Mount Lebanon, New York. The number indicated the color or weight of the wool, probably the latter. The Shakers also used large two-handled baskets to gather and store plant materials for their very successful pharmaceutical business. O.H. 12"; L. 29"; W. 22". Formerly in the collection of the Hon. Frank M. Reinhold.

PLATE 45. Shaker handled egg basket of hexagonal openwork weave: nineteenth century. The cheese curd baskets often thought of in connection with the Shakers, who sold them, were based on this weave. D. 6½"; Diam. 12". Photograph courtesy The Shaker Museum, Old Chatham, New York.

PLATE 46. Shaker basket, reputedly for carrying personal laundry to the Wash House: probably third quarter of the nineteenth century. Ash splint. This one may have come out of the Enfield, New Hampshire, community. O.H. 8¾″; L. 12″; W. 6¾″.

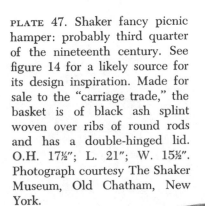

PLATE 47. Shaker fancy picnic hamper: probably third quarter of the nineteenth century. See figure 14 for a likely source for its design inspiration. Made for sale to the "carriage trade," the basket is of black ash splint woven over ribs of round rods and has a double-hinged lid. O.H. 17½"; L. 21"; W. 15½". Photograph courtesy The Shaker Museum, Old Chatham, New York.

PLATE 48. Group of old Nantucket Lightship Baskets offered for sale in 1973. Finely woven of rattan with turned-wood bases and movable handles. No maker has been identified for these baskets. Priced at several hundred dollars apiece, they represent our most valuable non-Indian type. The text discussion provides historical information. The oval basket at the right measures 10½" high with handle up; it is 13" long. Photograph courtesy Lawrence E. King, Monroe Center, Illinois.

PLATE 49. Nantucket Lightship Basket. Weavers of imported rattan, usual movable handle (the particular shape varied) attached to a pair of brass ears. Although durable, many of these baskets were treasured in their own time and saw service only as display pieces. O.H. 9½"; Diam. 7⅛". Photograph courtesy Lawrence E. King, Monroe Center, Illinois.

PLATE 50. Nantucket Lightship Basket with five concentric circles grooved into the turned-wood bottom: roughly dated between 1900 and 1930 but might be from the end of the nineteenth century. Experts differ about whether or not the number of grooved circles provides any valid clue to identification of the maker. Bases were often bought from others, a practice still followed, and the bases used by a weaver might bear different patterns as fancy dictated. Glued-on labels were used early, but many of them are now lost. Names burned into old ones may be those of owners, although present-day weavers usually do burn or carve their names into the bottom. H. handle 5"; D. 4¾"; Diam. 10".

PLATE 51. Pennsylvania German coiled rye-straw bread-raising/dough basket (often called "Mennonite baskets"): late nineteenth century. Note the hanger devised by pulling out a coil and binding it away from the construction; sometimes there are two, but usually there is none on these shallow, round or oval baskets that held the shaped loaves while they were left to rise overnight. Coiled-straw (other straws were used, but rye was preferred for its toughness and length) baskets turn up in former German communities elsewhere, where they were also made, and some are still being produced in Pennsylvania. D. 4¼"; Diam. 14".

PLATE 52. Coiled-straw baskets at the Pennsylvania Farm Museum of Landis Valley. Sometimes referred to as *beehive* baskets because European apiarists employed the construction to keep their bees from freezing in winter, they are associated with the Pennsylvania "Dutch," who relied upon them for storage. The large covered hamper (rear right) is called a *schnitz* basket because such bulbous forms held cheesecloth bags of dried apple segments, but they also did other storage duty. The large, flat mat (rear left) covered a distiller's vat and is 30" in diameter. Photograph courtesy the Pennsylvania Farm Museum of Landis Valley, Lancaster, Pennsylvania.

PLATE 53. Rib-type basket with double-splint handle. It was borrowed for a 1973 exhibition of The Art Institute of Chicago's collection of handwoven coverlets. Probably Pennsylvania: nineteenth century. O.H. 18"; L. 18¾". Photograph from The Art Institute of Chicago, permission courtesy the Pennsylvania Farm Museum of Landis Valley, Lancaster, Pennsylvania.

PLATE 54. Pair of flat-backed equine pack baskets (presumed): probably of American manufacture in the late eighteenth or early nineteenth century. Splint on rib-type construction. H. 14″; W. across back 20″. Photograph courtesy the Pennsylvania Farm Museum of Landis Valley, Lancaster, Pennsylvania.

PLATE 55. Football-shaped nut- or wool-gathering basket: nineteenth century. Unpeeled willow, one of a pair. Described in accession records as nut-gathering baskets, thrifty Canadian shepherds knew them as woolgathering baskets, into which they tucked bits of wool retrieved from thorny bushes and fences. H. 10⅛"; L. 16½". Photograph courtesy the Pennsylvania Farm Museum of Landis Valley, Lancaster, Pennsylvania.

PLATE 56. New white oak-splint baskets from Virginia. (Left) Square peck by Mr. and Mrs. William Cody Cook, formerly resident basketmakers at Colonial Williamsburg. O.H. 14¼"; L. 13½"; W. 10½". (Right) Covered sewing basket by Mr. Roy Black, an apprentice of the Cooks and one of two basket-makers now demonstrating there. O.H. 10"; Diam. 12½". These baskets are made in the manner of eighteenth-century service baskets. Splint is prepared by hand, using a knife to start the splints and to scrape and smooth them.

PLATE 57. Williamsburg basket with forked handle: probably made during the late 1960s, while Mr. and Mrs. William Cody Cook were resident basketmakers at Colonial Williamsburg. White oak splint. O.H. 13½"; L. 22"; W. 16". Photograph courtesy the Colonial Williamsburg Collection, Williamsburg, Virginia.

PLATE 58. Afro-American basket in close-up showing coiling, woven by Gullah-culture blacks of the Sea Islands region near Charleston, South Carolina. Purchased in 1950 from a woman vendor, who was assumed to be its maker, near Mount Pleasant. Materials are sweetgrass bundles sewn with strips of fresh green palmetto leaflets; the decorative darker band is of pine needles. H. 9½″; Diam. 11″. Photograph courtesy the Smithsonian Institution, Washington, D.C.

PLATE 59. Group of Gullah Afro-American baskets, collected north of Mount Pleasant near Charleston in 1974. Black women demonstrate the technique and sell from roadside stands along U. S. Highway 17. Coiled of sweet grass with palmetto-strip bindings and pine needles or rush added for decorative effect, these examples show strong African influence. Large covered

baskets are picnic hampers, with smaller versions of the one in the left foreground sold as sewing baskets or purse baskets. The two behind it are intended as wastebaskets or planters. The bowl in the foreground is particularly beautiful, its skilled maker having incorporated a dark gold rush. Tallest: H. with handle 23″; Diam. 12″.

PLATE 60. Recent Southern Appalachian Highlands basket forms of the usual white oak splint. The round basket (right rear) is a shallow form not previously encountered and is said to date from around 1900 but must be much more recent. Regardless of its intended function, it served as a maternity ward for the dealer's cat, who insisted upon littering her kittens in it. (Left front) Handled tray of rib-type construction, an earlier twentieth-century example of a form that continues in the region (older ones also come out

of the Northeast, especially Pennsylvania). (Left rear) Contemporary half-bushel rib-basket of the "splitting" type from West Virginia. (Right front) Today's Kentucky egg basket, woven by Golden ("Bunt") Howard. (Center) Rib-type with good lines (O.H. 12¼"; L. 15"; W. 7½") by a woman in her eighties who produces when she can. Most of the weavers (except among the North Carolina Cherokee) in the several-states area are quite elderly.

PLATE 61. Variations on rib-type construction, at least most of them from the Appalachians earlier in this century. This basic construction (shown in fig. 5) has been employed to produce sturdy baskets in countless variations. Perhaps the most interesting in the group is the one (center) of unpeeled willow, always much less usual in this region than splint, which is here used for a decorative band. The basket, which may be of Cherokee manufacture, displays the formerly common "folded square" where the all-around handle joins the rim. The handle, made of a heavy, peeled withe, has been brought out to the sides and flattened to stabilize the base. O.H. 13¾"; L. 18¾"; W. 14". The two at the left have under-rim openings for handling them.

PLATE 62. Rib-type covered picnic baskets, white oak splint. That at the right almost surely originated in the southern mountains earlier in the century; O.H. 15½″; L. 21½″; W. 12½″. The basket at the left was found in Missouri and is most likely Ozarks-made; O.H. 12¼″; L. 19″; W. 11½″.

PLATE 63. Carolina basket: twentieth-century design. White oak splint on rib-type construction. This modified circular form with continuously woven-in handle and flattened sides incorporates vegetal-dyed bands. The Cherokee make a knitting basket in this form, adding a "foot," an attached round splint base. H. 14″; W. 11½″; Across bottom 7″.

PLATE 64. Oriole: early twentieth century. White oak splint, rib-type construction, colored with native dyes, from Appalachia. The current name presumably comes from its resemblance to the oriole's hanging sacklike nest, but it was formerly called a Kentucky egg basket or jug basket (for its shape). One of the oldest forms in the region, it is still being made. Designed to hold eggs when traveling by horse or mule, either long, flattened side would lie smoothly against the animal's body, and the narrowed ovoid rim kept the contents from being jogged out. It is said that such baskets were once woven to hold exact dozens of eggs, a kind of measuring basket. O.H. 13¼"; At widest 7¾" x 9"; Top opening 6½ x 5½".

PLATE 65. Midwestern farm baskets: late nineteenth or early twentieth century. (Left rear) Simple but honest hickory splint from Illinois, a basket with many cousins. Note the outside splint straps, which extend all along the rectangular bottom and up the corners. The ash-splint flaring form (rear center) is a well-made basket from Ohio that bears generous traces of black paint. (Right rear) Ohio hickory splint with forked handle; a faded colored band and general construction appear Indian. (Left foreground) Nicely proportioned nailed-rim basket with checkerwork bottom and outcurved sides. (Right foreground) Horizontal-rib black ash basket of crude but strong structure, collected in Illinois. The only other example of this weave that I have seen was a 30"-long oval with hand openings under the rim that came from Indiana. O.H. 11"; L. 17¾"; W. 11".

PLATE 66. Willow-splint basket of twilled weave: nineteenth century. The weave and construction details, including traces of a dark dye on some weavers, all point to an Indian source. The work is reminiscent of that of Southeastern tribes, but the basket is of undetermined origin. O.H. 14"; Diam. 12". Photograph courtesy the Chicago Historical Society, Chicago, Illinois.

PLATE 67. Deep Ohio vegetable basket with copper-nailed rim: late nineteenth century. Of hickory, its superb craftsmanship includes a lapper to finish the rim; a utility basket that succeeds in being beautiful, too. O.H. 12¾"; Diam. 14½".

PLATE 68. Michigan apple basket: most likely third quarter of the nineteenth century. Hickory, red sumac stained. The inverted demijohn bottom carries the weight to the stronger outside edge. I have never seen a heavier basket, in construction or sheer weight. A basket for the ages! O.H. 14¼"; Diam. 21".

PLATE 69. Produce basket with five-inch-high raised bottom: nineteenth century. Raised centers protected fragile contents from being crushed by insuring a shallower depth in the middle and distributing part of the weight to the slightly flaring sides, at the same time protecting the weaker bottom from being pushed through by a heavy load when lifted or dragged along. This is the highest raised bottom I have seen, but its particular purpose is unknown. H. 13"; Diam. 13". Photograph courtesy the Chicago Historical Society, Chicago, Illinois.

PLATE 70. Pike County (Illinois) barrel basket, so named by the dealer who collected it there. Reputed to be ninety years old, it closely resembles one purchased from an Ozarks basketmaking family in the 1930s or 1940s. Covered and doubtless intended as a hamper for soiled laundry, the shape is more that of a somewhat flattened egg, and it has become lopsided through years of service and casual care. Baskets can get badly out of shape if left lying on their sides, overloaded, especially when damp, or left hanging in leaky barns. H. 25″; Diam. 16″.

PLATE 71. Heavy peeled-willow basket for wholesale meat delivery: used in Chicago during the earliest years of this century. It must have taken very strong hands to weave this basket. Others had handles at the ends so that two men could carry a hundred pounds. O.H. 20½″; L. 28″; W. 16″.

PLATE 72. Creel-shaped two-legged basket with pine cover: hand-forged iron hinges date it as nineteenth century. Found in Nebraska, the name on the lid, "A. L. Karlsjon," a Scandinavian spelling, suggests ownership by an immigrant who may have brought it with him to the "New Land." O.H. 18"; L. 17"; W. 15".

PLATE 73. Baskets from the Amana Colonies of Iowa. (Left to right) Field basket of unpeeled willow (O.H. 13¾"; Diam. 22"); Shoup basket from South Amana, a splint (poplar?) form unique to one weaver and made for his personal uses; communion-bread basket (*liebesbrot*) of peeled willow; handled market or shopping basket from West Amana, alternating weavers of peeled and unpeeled willow, those of each kind passed over and under the same ribs to achieve vertical bands of dark and light. The Shoup basket is well over a hundred years old, the *liebesbrot* over a hundred, the market basket probably somewhat younger, and the field basket from early in this century. It has been turned on its side to exhibit the base border distinctive to Amana wickerwork baskets, which protected the bottom and was easily replaceable when damaged so the basket could be quickly returned to service.

PLATE 74. New Ozarks white oak-splint baskets. The half-bushel (left rear) (O.H. 16½"; Diam. 20") and the "one-pie" food carrier (far right), of which variations are woven to accommodate different dishes, are from the Gibson family of northwestern Arkansas. The deep basket with base border (rarely found elsewhere today) and the cone-shaped basket with hanging loop—to hold "pretties," candles, or kitchen utensils—are by Woody Gannaway of Mountain View, a talented young weaver innovating within the traditional medium. The small basket with heart-shaped handle (left) is by Herschal Hall, also of Mountain View. In Arkansas, squared bottoms are twill-plaited and the handles typically well carved and notched to fit around the rim hoop. Rib-type baskets are not being made in that state, but at least one couple in Missouri, third-generation basketmakers, produce round and oval handled baskets similar to the picnic hamper at the left in plate 62.

Selected
Bibliography

BENNETT, ETHEL. *Splint Basket Making*. Agricultural Extension Service: University of Arkansas Division of Agriculture and U.S. Department of Agriculture, Cooperating, April, 1967.

CHASE, JUDITH WRAGG. *Afro-American Art & Craft*. New York: Van Nostrand Reinhold Company, 1971.

CHRISTOPHER, F. J. *Basketry*. New York: Dover Publications, Inc., 1952 (an unabridged and slightly revised republication of the work originally published in 1951 by W. & G. Foyle, Ltd.).

DOCKSTADER, FREDERICK J. *Indian Art in North America—Arts & Crafts*. Greenwich, Conn.: New York Graphic Society, retitled reprinting of *Indian Art in America: The Arts & Crafts of the North American Indian*, 1961.

EATON, ALLEN H. *Handicrafts of New England*. New York: Bonanza Books, a division of Crown Publishers, Inc., by arrangement with Harper & Row, 1969 (orig. ed. Harper and Brothers, 1949).

————. *Handicrafts of the Southern Highlands*. New York: Dover Publications, Inc., 1973 (an unabridged republication of the work originally published in 1937 by Russell Sage Foundation, New York).

ELLIOT, JAMES. "Shaker Collecting." *Maine Antique Digest* (April 1974).

FLAYDERMAN, E. NORMAN. *Scrimshaw and Scrimshanders: Whales and Whalemen.* New Milford, Conn.: N. Flayderman & Co., Inc., 1972, pp. 280–288 ("Nantucket Lightship Baskets").

FOREMAN, LOUISE. "Preserve and Protect Your American Indian Baskets." *The Masterkey,* Vol. 45, No. 2 (April–June 1971). Southwest Museum, Highland Park, Los Angeles.

GOULD, MARY EARLE. *Early American Wooden Ware & Other Kitchen Utensils.* Springfield, Mass.: The Pond-Ekberg Company, 1942.

HOPF, CARROLL J. "Basketware of the Northeast: A Survey of the Types of Basketware Used on the Farm from the Colonial Period to 1860." Thesis submitted to the faculty of State University of New York College at Oneonta, at its Cooperstown Graduate Programs, 1965.

JAMES, GEORGE WHARTON. *Indian Basketry.* New York: Dover Publications, Inc., 1972 (an unabridged and unaltered republication of the fourth edition of *Indian Basketry* published in 1909 by Henry Malkan).

KETCHUM, WILLIAM C., JR. *American Basketry and Woodenware.* New York: Macmillan Publishing Co., Inc.; and London, England: Collier Macmillan Publishers, 1974.

KLAMKIN, MARIAN. *Hands to Work: Shaker Folk Art and Industries.* New York: Dodd, Mead & Company, 1972.

LAMB, DR. FRANK W. *Indian Baskets of North America.* Riverside, Calif.: Riverside Museum Press, 1972.

LEFTWICH, RODNEY L. *Arts and Crafts of the Cherokee.* Cullowhee, N.C.: Land-of-the-Sky Press, 1970.

LISMER, MARJORIE. *Seneca Splint Basketry.* Chilocco, Okla.: Education Division, U.S. Office of Indian Affairs, 1941.

LYFORD, CARRIE A. *The Crafts of the Ojibwa (Chippewa).* Phoenix, Ariz.: Education Division, U.S. Office of Indian Affairs, 1943.

MASON, OTIS TUFTON. "Aboriginal American Basketry: Studies in a Textile Art Without Machinery." *Annual Report of the Smithsonian Institution.* Report of the United States National Museum. Washington, D.C.: 1902, pp. 171–548 and Pls. 1–248.

MEILACH, DONA Z. *A Modern Approach to Basketry with Fibers and Grasses (Using Coiling, Twining, Weaving, Macramé, Crocheting).* New York: Crown Publishers, Inc., 1974.

MILES, CHARLES, and BOVIS, PIERRE. *American Indian and Eskimo Basketry: A Key to Identification.* New York: Bonanza Books, a division of Crown Publishers, Inc., 1969.

NAVAJO SCHOOL OF BASKETRY, THE. *Indian Basket Weaving.* New York: Dover Publications, Inc., 1971 (an unabridged republication of the work originally published in 1903 by Whedon & Spreng Co., Los Angeles).

NEWMAN, SANDRA CORRIE. *Indian Basket Weaving: How to Weave Pomo, Yurok, Pima and Navajo Baskets.* Flagstaff, Ariz.: Northland Press, 1974.

REINERT, GUY F. *Pennsylvania German Splint and Straw Baskets.* Home Craft Course, Vol. 22. Plymouth Meeting, Pa.: Mrs. C. Naaman Keyser, 1946.

ROBACKER, EARL F. *Touch of the Dutchland.* New York: A. S. Barnes and Company, 1965.

——. *Old Stuff in Up-Country Pennsylvania.* South Brunswick, N.J., and New York: A. S. Barnes and Company; London, England: Thomas Yoseloff Ltd., 1973.

ROBINSON, BERT. *The Basket Weavers of Arizona.* Albuquerque, N.M.: University of New Mexico Press, 1954.

ROSSBACH, ED. *Baskets as Textile Art.* New York: Van Nostrand Reinhold Company, 1973.

SEELER, KATHERINE, and SEELER, EDGAR. *Nantucket Lightship Baskets.* Nantucket, Mass.: The Deermouse Press, 1972.

TANNER, CLARA LEE. *Southwest Indian Craft Arts.* Tucson, Ariz.: University of Arizona Press, 1968.

TOD, OSMA GALLINGER. *Earth Basketry.* New York: Bonanza Books, a division of Crown Publishers, Inc., 1972.

WEYGANDT, CORNELIUS. *The Dutch Country.* New York: D. Appleton-Century Company, Inc., 1939.

WHITEFORD, ANDREW HUNTER. *North American Indian Arts.* New York: Golden Press, Western Publishing Company, Inc., 1970.

WIGGINTON, ELIOT, ed. *The Foxfire Book.* New York: Anchor Books, Doubleday & Company, Inc., 1972.

Index